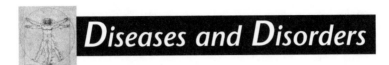

Diseases and Disorders

Cerebral
Palsy

Titles in the Diseases and Disorders series include:

Alzheimer's Disease
Anorexia and Bulimia
Arthritis
Asthma
Attention Deficit Disorder
Autism
Breast Cancer
Chronic Fatigue Syndrome
Cystic Fibrosis
Diabetes
Down Syndrome
Epilepsy
Hemophilia
Hepatitis
Learning Disabilities
Leukemia
Lyme Disease
Multiple Sclerosis
Phobias
Schizophrenia
Sleep Disorders

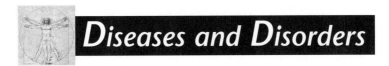

Diseases and Disorders

Cerebral Palsy

by Barbara Sheen

LUCENT BOOKS®

THOMSON

—————TM

GALE

San Diego • Detroit • New York • San Francisco • Cleveland
New Haven, Conn. • Waterville, Maine • London • Munich

LIBRARY OF CONGRESS CATALOGING-IN-PUBLICATION DATA

Sheen, Barbara.
  Cerebral palsy / by Barbara Sheen.
     p. cm.— (Diseases and disorders series)
Includes bibliographical references and index.
Summary: Discusses and describes cerebral palsy, its treatments,
and the future of technological treatments for the disease.
  ISBN 1-59018-038-0 (hdbk.: alk. paper)
  1. Cerebral palsy—Juvenile literature. [1. Cerebral palsy. 2. Diseases.]
I.Title. II. Diseases and disorders series.
RC388 .S435 2004
616.8'36—dc21
                                                                    2002153659

Printed in the United States of America

Table of Contents

"The Most Difficult Puzzles Ever Devised"

CHARLES BEST, ONE of the pioneers in the search for a cure for diabetes, once explained what it is about medical research that intrigued him so. "It's not just the gratification of knowing one is helping people," he confided, "although that probably is a more heroic and selfless motivation. Those feelings may enter in, but truly, what I find best is the feeling of going toe to toe with nature, of trying to solve the most difficult puzzles ever devised. The answers are there somewhere, those keys that will solve the puzzle and make the patient well. But how will those keys be found?"

Since the dawn of civilization, nothing has so puzzled people—and often frightened them, as well—as the onset of illness in a body or mind that had seemed healthy before. A seizure, the inability of a heart to pump, the sudden deterioration of muscle tone in a small child—being unable to reverse such conditions or even to understand why they occur was unspeakably frustrating to healers. Even before there were names for such conditions, even before they were understood at all, each was a reminder of how complex the human body was, and how vulnerable.

While our grappling with understanding diseases has been frustrating at times, it has also provided some of humankind's most heroic accomplishments. Alexander Fleming's accidental discovery in 1928 of a mold that could be turned into penicillin has resulted in the saving of untold millions of lives. The isolation of the enzyme insulin has reversed what was once a death sentence for anyone with diabetes. There have been great strides in combating conditions for which there is not yet a cure, too. Medicines can help AIDS patients live longer, diagnostic tools such as mammography and ultrasounds can help doctors find tumors while they are treatable, and laser surgery techniques have made the most intricate, minute operations routine.

This "toe-to-toe" competition with diseases and disorders is even more remarkable when seen in a historical continuum. An astonishing amount of progress has been made in a very short time. Just two hundred years ago, the existence of germs as a cause of some diseases was unknown. In fact, it was less than 150 years ago that a British surgeon named Joseph Lister had difficulty persuading his fellow doctors that washing their hands before delivering a baby might increase the chances of a healthy delivery (especially if they had just attended to a diseased patient)!

Each book in Lucent's Diseases and Disorders series explores a disease or disorder and the knowledge that has been accumulated (or discarded) by doctors through the years. Each book also examines the tools used for pinpointing a diagnosis, as well as the various means that are used to treat or cure a disease. Finally, new ideas are presented—techniques or medicines that may be on the horizon.

Frustration and disappointment are still part of medicine, for not every disease or condition can be cured or prevented. But the limitations of knowledge are being pushed outward constantly; the "most difficult puzzles ever devised" are finding challengers every day.

A Misunderstood Disorder

WHEN AMANDA WAS a year old, her parents realized that there was something wrong with her. Not only had she not started walking yet, but she could neither sit up straight nor stand. And when she crawled, she pulled herself along with her hands. Amanda's doctor agreed that she was not developing at a normal rate. After examining her and administering a number of tests, the doctor diagnosed her with cerebral palsy. Amanda explains how the diagnosis affected her parents:

> Although there'd been problems at my birth, they never expected I'd wind up with cerebral palsy [CP]. The worst part was that they didn't know what to expect, and no one could give them answers. They didn't know if I'd ever be able to walk, or use my arms, or talk. They didn't know if I'd ever be able to become an independent adult. Not even the doctor could take a guess, because CP affects every person differently. My parents went home and started reading up on CP. They figured that even if they couldn't predict what would happen to me, they needed to know why it was happening and what they could do about it.[1]

Amanda's parents soon learned that cerebral palsy is a serious disorder that affects people's control of their muscles. Usually caused by an injury to the brain before, during, or shortly after birth, cerebral palsy affects a wide range of physical functions, including walking, using one's hands and arms, speaking, and swallowing. Amanda and her parents are not alone. One in every

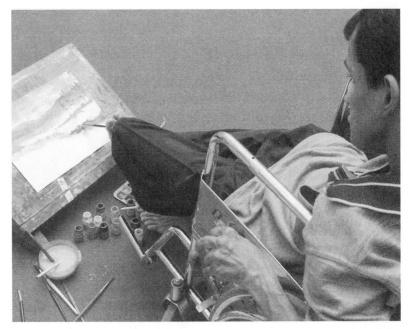

A determined artist afflicted with cerebral palsy masters his craft, despite his disability, by painting with his toes.

thousand babies born in the United States is diagnosed with cerebral palsy, and despite improvements in health care, these numbers have not changed significantly over the last fifty years. In fact, some experts believe that improvements in health care have actually contributed to the number of cases rising slightly. The reason for this is infants who would not have survived in the past are surviving through improved health care. Many of these babies have a number of developmental problems, however, which often results in the development of cerebral palsy. As a result, approximately seven hundred thousand Americans have some form of cerebral palsy, making it among the most common permanent disabilities in the United States.

Physically Different, Emotionally the Same

Yet despite the large number of people who suffer from cerebral palsy and the difficulties it imposes on their lives, many people with cerebral palsy say that their biggest problem is not their disability but, rather, the way other people treat them. According to Amanda,

> When people first meet me, they can't seem to get beyond my disability. They don't see the person I am. All they see is my disability and my wheelchair, and they treat me differently. Although my body doesn't work right, my mind does. But most people don't realize it. They can't believe that I'm the vice president of my senior class and an honor roll student, or that I'm getting ready to go to college. And they're amazed to find out I have my driver's license and my own specially equipped car. Being disabled isn't the same as being unable, and people need to understand that. It seems like people with disabilities always have to prove themselves in order to be treated like everyone else. And that really makes having CP even harder. If I had one wish it would be that people understand that there's a person inside this body that doesn't work, and they need to give me, and people like me, a chance.[2]

An ecstatic youngster with CP water-skis on special equipment. Two men follow to ensure his safety.

When given a chance, people with cerebral palsy are able to accomplish many things. Many people with cerebral palsy are college graduates with successful careers and happy families. They are also stand-up comics, artists, lawyers, teachers, and business owners.

In order to give people with cerebral palsy a chance, it is important that people understand more about the disorder. By learning more about cerebral palsy and how it affects the body, people will gain a better understanding of what it is like to have the disorder. With this understanding, they will become more sensitive about the way they interact with people with cerebral palsy. At the same time, by learning how to treat cerebral palsy and the challenges it presents, friends and family members will gain a better understanding of how to provide cerebral palsy patients with appropriate support. Moreover, people with cerebral palsy and their families will be able to make better choices about their treatment and learn ways to manage their disorder.

At nineteen, Amanda and her family have learned quite a bit about cerebral palsy and how to manage it. Amanda is a busy and popular high school senior with dreams of becoming a fashion designer. Although the road to reaching her dreams may be harder for Amanda than it is for other people, Amanda is confident that she can make those dreams come true. "I believe in myself," she explains. "When you have a disability you have to work harder sometimes, and you have to prove yourself. But that doesn't mean you can't live a normal life. I plan to go to college, have a career, get married, and be an awesome mom. Having CP will make it harder, but not impossible."[3]

Chapter 1

What Is Cerebral Palsy?

CEREBRAL PALSY IS a disabling disorder of the brain's motor centers. Whereas most people can will their bodies to move in the myriad ways that allow them to throw a ball or jump rope, people with cerebral palsy are unable to control their movements. Cerebral palsy results from damage to the brain's motor centers, and depending on the degree of damage, the disability a person experiences may range from minor to incapacitating.

What Type of Condition Is Cerebral Palsy?

Cerebral palsy is what doctors call an incurable static, or unchanging, disorder. What this means is that, unlike many diseases, once people develop cerebral palsy, they have it for the rest of their lives. Furthermore, their movement impairments will neither worsen nor improve. A young man with cerebral palsy explains what it is like to have a static disorder that has caused him to be permanently disabled: "When you have a cold or a cough, you feel sick for a while, but eventually you get better. When you have CP, you never get better. At least you don't get worse, either. My right side is disabled. It's been the same way since I was little. It will always be this way, even when I'm an old man."[4]

What Causes Cerebral Palsy?

Cerebral palsy results from damage to the brain that causes brain cells to develop improperly. This occurs before, during, or shortly after birth. This damage, in turn, can be caused by a number of events, such as lack of oxygen, bleeding in the brain,

Most cases of CP appear very early in a life, sometimes while an infant is still in the mother's womb.

or the incompatibility of a chemical known as the Rh factor in the mother's and baby's blood. However, the exact sequence of events is unknown, as is which brain cells are affected.

Limited oxygen supply is one event that is often linked to cerebral palsy. The brain depends on a constant supply of oxygen to function normally. If the brain receives an inadequate supply of oxygen, even for a short time, it can damage brain cells. In the case of newborn babies, this can also keep brain cells from developing normally. If the brain cells that are damaged control movement, the result is often cerebral palsy.

Lack of oxygen most commonly occurs during birth because of the length of the labor or because of problems in the birth canal that restrict the baby's oxygen supply. A patient explains what happened to her:

> After twenty hours of labor, mom knew that the pain she was experiencing was not normal. Mom's narrow pelvis had prevented my head from entering the birth canal. I experienced lack of oxygen for about five minutes. The doctor revived me.

Six months after my birth, I had difficulty rolling to my side when I was lying in my crib. The diagnosis was cerebral palsy.[5]

Bleeding in the brain, or a stroke, which sometimes occurs in the fetus or in newborn infants around the time of birth, is another event that scientists think may cause cerebral palsy. Strokes can be caused by clogged or broken blood vessels in the developing brain of a fetus. Scientists do not know why this occurs. However, they agree that bleeding in the brain puts pressure on fragile brain cells, causing them to rupture or break. If the brain cells affected are those that control movement, cerebral palsy may occur.

Another circumstance that scientists think can lead to cerebral palsy occurs when babies are born with a protein in their blood called the Rh factor, that their mothers do not have. When this happens, the mother's blood produces antibodies that attack the fetus's red blood cells, where the Rh factor is carried. When too

CP can be triggered by the interruption of an infant's oxygen supply at birth, Rh incompatibility with its mother, or a stroke.

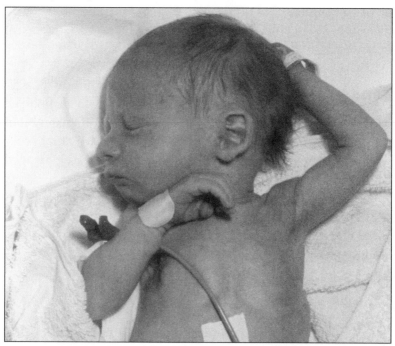

many red blood cells are destroyed in this manner, a powerful chemical known as bilirubin can build up in the blood. High levels of bilirubin can damage brain cells that control movement.

Types of Cerebral Palsy

No matter what causes cerebral palsy, exactly how movement is impaired depends on how many and which brain cells have been damaged. Cerebral palsy symptoms, therefore, vary widely from person to person. Despite this variability, doctors classify cerebral palsy into four main types based on how movement is affected. These types are spastic, athetoid, ataxic, and mixed cerebral palsy.

Of the four types of cerebral palsy, the most common is spastic. It affects 80 percent of all people with the disorder. When people have spastic cerebral palsy, their muscles are tight and contracted. No matter how hard people with spastic cerebral palsy try, they are unable to relax the affected muscles. People with spastic cerebral palsy may not be able to extend their arm or unclench their fist, and this often causes pain. A mother of a child with spastic cerebral palsy explains what this type of muscle tension feels like: "I asked his therapist if he [her son] was in pain. She suggested an activity that would give me an idea how his legs might feel. She told me to bend my arm at the elbow, in towards me and hold it until it shakes. After a few minutes my arm began to cramp. I then released my arm and held it out straight. I could feel the tension in my muscles."[6] In addition, since stiff muscles cannot bend easily, this stiffness also causes people with spastic cerebral palsy to move in a jerky, almost scissors-like manner.

Whereas spastic cerebral palsy limits motion, athetoid cerebral palsy, which affects about 10 percent of all people with the disorder, causes excessive, uncontrollable motion. When people have athetoid cerebral palsy, their muscles move involuntarily. This causes their limbs to jerk, twitch, or flay uncontrollably. A patient explains, "My athetosis [athetoid cerebral palsy] causes occasional uncontrollable muscle movements, especially in my hands. I often knock something over or hit people with my hands unintentionally."[7]

Another 10 percent of cerebral palsy patients have what is called ataxic cerebral palsy. People with ataxic cerebral palsy have problems with balance and coordination. They appear clumsy when they walk and are unable to stand in one place without falling over. These patients also have poor eye-hand coordination. They can see where they want to move, but they have trouble making their limbs move in the desired direction. This makes activities like being able to write, grasping eating utensils, or dressing oneself difficult.

Some people with cerebral palsy have symptoms of more than one form of the disorder. This is known as mixed cerebral palsy. For example, a person might have spastic muscle movements in one part of his or her body and athetoid movements in another part. Although any of the three forms of cerebral palsy can be present in mixed cerebral palsy, the most common combination is spastic and athetoid cerebral palsy.

Classification by Disabled Body Parts

All four types of cerebral palsy can affect a variety of muscles. Some people may have many muscles affected, but others may have only a few. For this reason, doctors further classify cerebral palsy according to the body parts affected. For example, when a patient has movement problems in one arm and one leg on one side of the body, this is known as hemiplegia. When both legs are affected, this is called diplegia, and when all four limbs are disabled, this is called quadriplegia.

These classifications are often combined with the type of cerebral palsy patients have in order to better describe how cerebral palsy affects their body. For example, people with spastic cerebral palsy that affects one side of the body are said to have spastic hemiplegia. When both their legs are affected, they have spastic diplegia. If all their limbs are affected, they have spastic quadriplegia. Athetoid and ataxic cerebral palsy are similarly classified. A patient explains what his particular form of cerebral palsy means in practical terms: "I have spastic hemiplegia. This means my right arm and leg are very stiff and hard to control. I drag my right leg when I walk, and my right arm is, pretty much, useless. But my left arm and leg work just fine."[8]

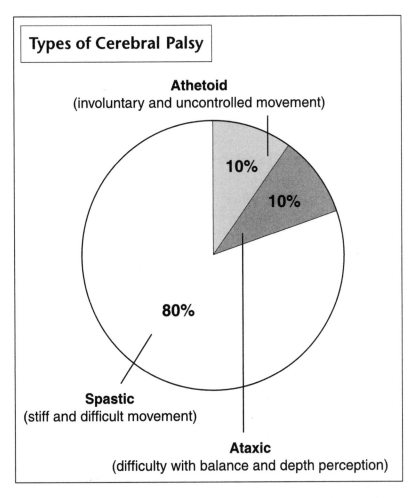

Types of Cerebral Palsy

Athetoid
(involuntary and uncontrolled movement)

10%

10%

80%

Spastic
(stiff and difficult movement)

Ataxic
(difficulty with balance and depth perception)

Just as cerebral palsy impacts different muscles in different patients, so does the disorder's severity differ from one individual to the next. Cerebral palsy can be mild, moderate, or severe. In mild cases, patients may move awkwardly but otherwise seem perfectly normal. People with moderate cases may have trouble walking or using their arms easily. People with severe cases, on the other hand, may be unable to walk, use their arms, or even hold their neck and head erect. A patient with a severe case explains, "I cannot talk, walk, or use my hands. I communicate with an electronic communication device. I use a motorized wheelchair, which I control with pressure from the back of my head."[9]

People at Risk

Although the problems that cause cerebral palsy can arise in anyone, there are certain factors that put some newborn babies at greater risk of developing the disorder. One such factor occurs when pregnant mothers are infected with certain viruses or bacteria that injure their unborn baby's brain. These include the rubella or German measles virus, toxoplasmosis bacteria, which is found in cat feces, and the cytomegalovirus, which can infect raw and undercooked meat. Scientists are unsure why these particular organisms affect brain cell development in such a negative way. However, they are sure that pregnant women who are not vaccinated against rubella, those who in some way are exposed to cat feces, and those who habitually eat meat that has not been cooked to at least medium-well done run a significant risk of having a child with cerebral palsy.

Unhealthy Living and Poor Nutrition

Another risk associated with cerebral palsy is the use of drugs, alcohol, and cigarettes by the expectant mother. Chemicals that

A premature baby is treated in an incubator. A birth weight of less than five pounds may put a baby at risk of developing CP.

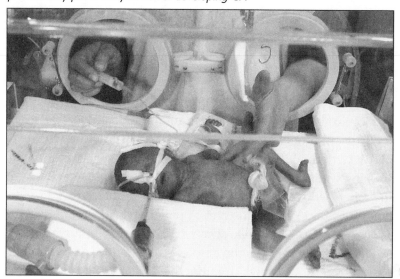

enter an expectant mother's bloodstream by whatever means are eventually passed to her fetus through the placenta; and some chemicals, such as nicotine and alcohol, can stunt or otherwise negatively affect the growth of brain cells. Other drugs, such as cocaine and crack, are known to cause hemorrhaging, or bleeding, in the brains of fetuses exposed to them. According to cerebral palsy expert Dr. Freeman Miller, "The use of cocaine or crack by the expectant mother is associated with blood vessel complications . . . .and is becoming more prevalent as a cause of brain damage in infants."[10]

Malnutrition of the mother-to-be is yet another risk factor in the development of cerebral palsy. Chronic malnutrition literally starves developing brain cells in the fetus and can lead to abnormal development.

Low Birth Weight and Premature Birth

Poor nutrition also leads to babies being born weighing under five pounds. This is much lower than the average birth weight of seven pounds. Such small babies are often weak and unhealthy, and their brains have not received sufficient nutrition to grow and develop normally. As a result, low-birth-weight babies are at risk of developing cerebral palsy. In fact, statistics show that babies who weigh less than three pounds at birth are twenty-five times more likely to develop cerebral palsy than babies weighing five or more pounds.

Many low-birth-weight babies are also born prematurely, and premature birth is another risk associated with cerebral palsy. The reason for this is that premature babies are cut off from the support their mothers provide before they are fully developed. Consequently, premature babies do not have ample time for all their body systems, including their brains, to grow and develop adequately. This can lead to a number of problems. Among these are inadequately developed brains and lungs, which often lead to breathing problems and the baby receiving insufficient oxygen. A young woman with cerebral palsy who was born prematurely describes her experience: "I was born two and a half months premature. I weighed only three pounds, twelve ounces and was immediately put on a respirator [a machine that helps a person breathe]. Among the most serious of my many problems were collapsed lungs and veins."[11]

Head Injuries

Not all factors that put a baby at risk of developing cerebral palsy are present before or immediately after birth. Blows to the head that occur within the first six months of an infant's life may also lead to cerebral palsy. This is because the skull, which protects the brain, is still somewhat soft and pliable in infants. Therefore, any head trauma, whether from a fall, a car accident, or child abuse, can damage the brain. In the United States, between 10 and 20 percent of all cases of cerebral palsy are caused by head injury as an infant.

Unknown Risk Factors

Although babies who experience any of these risk factors are more likely to develop cerebral palsy, the disorder can strike anyone. It affects males and females of every race. And although doctors often know what factors cause cerebral palsy, in some cases the cause is unknown and infants who do not experience any of the risk factors still develop the disorder. Experts estimate that this is the circumstance in approximately 20 percent of all cases of cerebral palsy. This has led doctors to think that perhaps there are other factors, such as environmental factors like exposure to air pollutants and secondhand smoke or dietary factors, such as vitamin or mineral deficiencies, that can put an infant at risk. Consequently, much about cerebral palsy still remains a mystery.

The Physical Impact of Cerebral Palsy

No matter what factors cause people to develop cerebral palsy, the disorder has a large physical impact on the body. In addition to affecting people's arms, legs, and neck, cerebral palsy often affects a person's speech. Lack of muscle control in the tongue, vocal cords, mouth, and lungs can interfere with a person's breath control, tongue, vocal cords, and mouth movement, all of which are necessary to be able to speak clearly. Consequently, many

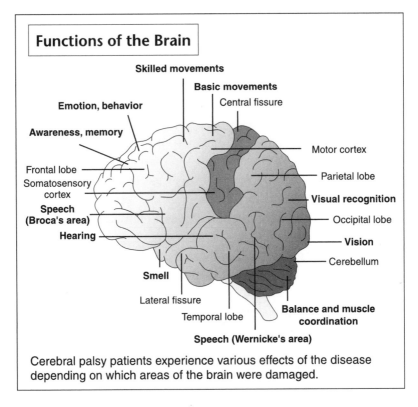

Functions of the Brain

Skilled movements

Basic movements

Emotion, behavior

Central fissure

Awareness, memory

Motor cortex

Frontal lobe

Parietal lobe

Somatosensory cortex

Visual recognition

Speech (Broca's area)

Occipital lobe

Hearing

Vision

Cerebellum

Smell

Lateral fissure

Balance and muscle coordination

Temporal lobe

Speech (Wernicke's area)

Cerebral palsy patients experience various effects of the disease depending on which areas of the brain were damaged.

people with cerebral palsy have speech problems. These problems may cause patients to slur words or be unable to produce certain sounds. This makes it difficult for them to communicate and often leaves them socially isolated. When speech problems are severe, people with cerebral palsy may not be able to speak at all.

Lack of muscle control in the mouth can also cause people with cerebral palsy to drool or have trouble swallowing food. When people cannot control the muscles in their mouths, they often have problems swallowing their saliva. When this happens, their mouths fill with saliva, and having nowhere to go, the saliva spills out onto the patient's face and chin. About 35 percent of people with cerebral palsy have problems with drooling. In addition, problems swallowing can make it difficult for people with cerebral palsy to swallow food. When this happens, people must be fed with special feeding tubes that allow food to pass directly into the patient's esophagus.

Associated Problems

In addition to the symptoms of cerebral palsy itself, people with the disorder frequently experience other problems that result from the brain damage that caused cerebral palsy. Brain cells responsible for other brain functions are frequently damaged as well. Consequently, people with cerebral palsy often have a number of associated problems. Such problems commonly include seizures, poor eyesight, learning disabilities, and mental retardation.

Seizures are the most common of these associated problems. Seizures occur when synapses, the normal electrical connections within the brain, are disrupted. Experts think that seizures are the result of scarred tissue in the brain. And since as many as 50 percent of people with cerebral palsy suffer from seizures, many experts believe that the same cell damage that causes cerebral palsy is also responsible for seizures.

Nearly half of all people with cerebral palsy also have visual problems. These problems are most common in people with hemiplegia. For example, muscle control problems, in a person's right side may include problems with the muscles that control the right

A mask protects an infant's eyes during phototherapy, a treatment designed to reverse jaundice.

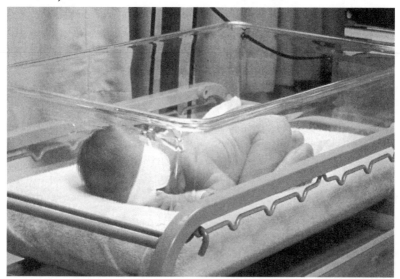

eye. As a result, many of these people have normal muscle control in one eye and weak muscle control in the other. This can make it difficult for the affected eye to move from side to side. As a result, people with this problem appear to have crossed eyes and often have very poor vision in the affected eye. A patient explains, "The muscles in my right eye are weak. This made my eye turn inward. I had surgery when I was little to loosen up the muscles. That helped. But I still don't see all that well out of my right eye."[12]

Another problem people with cerebral palsy often have is learning disabilities. People with learning disabilities have normal intelligence, but problems in their brains cause them to have difficulty learning. These difficulties may involve their ability to read, write, spell, or do mathematical calculations. Scientists think this occurs because the same processes that lead to cerebral palsy sometimes also damage cells that process visual data or spatial relationships.

Sometimes, too, the processes that damage brain cells and cause cerebral palsy damage brain cells in the cerebrum, the part of the brain that controls intelligence and thinking. When this happens, mental retardation can result. In fact, such damage is common enough that approximately two-thirds of people with cerebral palsy also are mentally retarded. The extent of their mental retardation ranges from mild to severe.

A Preventable Disorder

Although experts recognize that a small percentage of cases of cerebral palsy occur for no discernible reason, scientists believe that they have a good understanding of many of the risk factors and causes of the disorder. With this understanding comes the hope of preventing the vast majority of cases. Experts, for example, advise mothers-to-be to avoid use of drugs, cigarettes, and alcohol, all of which can damage brain cells in the developing fetus. Doctors also stress the benefits of paying careful attention to nutrition during pregnancy. According to cerebral palsy experts at the Neurology Channel, a medical website that deals with nervous system disorders, "The best prescription for having a healthy baby is to have regular prenatal care and good nutrition, and to avoid smoking, alcohol consumption and drug abuse. A pregnancy marked by these conditions is less likely to result in birth complications and problems in the newborn."[13]

Doctors also emphasize the importance of mothers' avoiding diseases that may lead to cerebral palsy in their babies. For example, doctors urge expectant mothers to get immunized against rubella, which keeps mothers from getting measles and lowers their babies' risk of developing cerebral palsy. They also warn expectant mothers to avoid contact with cat feces or raw meat, both of which spread germs that cause cerebral palsy.

Doctors also stress the importance of good prenatal and postnatal care. Blood tests can detect Rh factor incompatibility, for example, and steps can be taken to counteract any problems before the damage occurs. Similarly, treatments are widely available to reverse jaundice and prevent bilirubin from building up and damaging cells in the baby's brain.

Once a newborn leaves the hospital, responsibility for preventing cerebral palsy becomes a matter of taking steps to prevent head trauma. For example, most states require that babies riding in a car be securely strapped in special safety seats. Parents need to be constantly vigilant to prevent falls that can result in head injury or any other mishap that might result in injury to the highly vulnerable brain of the young child.

Yet despite all the efforts of prevention, cases of cerebral palsy can and do occur. For those individuals who develop cerebral palsy, or for those closest to them, the early challenge is recognizing the symptoms of the disorder and then dealing with them.

Chapter 2

Diagnosis and Treatment

O VER THE YEARS, doctors have developed a great deal of knowledge about cerebral palsy. Still, diagnosing cerebral palsy can be difficult and time-consuming. Moreover, no cure yet exists for the condition. Instead, once cerebral palsy is diagnosed, treatment is tailored to each individual's needs to help the patient live as productively as possible.

No Blood Test

Diagnosing cerebral palsy is an inexact process. There is, for example, no blood test for cerebral palsy, and even the most sophisticated devices, such as magnetic resonance imaging (MRI) or computerized axial tomography (CAT) scanners, cannot detect the damaged cells that cause symptoms. Instead, when cerebral palsy is suspected, doctors must examine patients and question parents to see if they have noted any delays in the child's expected development. Doctors also check the child's muscles to see if they feel stiff and tight or loose and floppy. Stiff muscles indicate the possibility of spastic cerebral palsy, and loose, floppy muscles point to athetoid cerebral palsy. Next, the child's reflexes are examined to see if they respond normally when they are stimulated. Then, the doctor compares the child's physical development and muscle control with what is considered normal for children of the same age. At the same time, since symptoms of cerebral palsy closely resemble those of other ailments, doctors must eliminate brain tumors, severe allergies, muscular dystrophy, arthritis, and various cancers as possible explanations.

What usually confirms the diagnosis is whether the symptoms worsen. Since cerebral palsy is a static disorder that does not improve or worsen, monitoring patients over a few months helps doctors determine whether the cause of a child's symptoms is cerebral palsy.

Motor Skills

The first indications of cerebral palsy are usually a child's failure to acquire particular motor skills when his or her peers do. These skills include securely holding his or her head up, rolling over, sitting, crawling, and walking. Although each child develops at a different pace, doctors become concerned when these skills are seriously delayed. Such delays include a child's inability to hold his or her head up by three months, roll over by eight months, sit independently by ten months, crawl by one year, and walk by three years.

Usually, the parent is the first to become concerned. One mother talks about delays in her daughter's development:

> Unlike her older sister, she was late in developing. But since she was born prematurely, I thought maybe the problems she had at birth might have slowed her down. But when she still couldn't sit up by herself at her first birthday party, I started getting concerned. We had to prop her up with pillows to get her to sit, and she still listed to the side. When she wasn't crawling when she was two, my concern turned to fear. I knew there was something wrong, and I was right. She had cerebral palsy.[14]

Finding Associated Problems

Once other possible causes of a child's symptoms have been eliminated and cerebral palsy is diagnosed, the doctor tries to determine the type of cerebral palsy involved. The doctor determines this by examining the patient's muscle tone and the patient's ability to control different parts of his or her body. Then, the doctor tries to determine whether the patient has associated problems, resulting from the brain damage that caused cerebral palsy. For example, the doctor may order a CAT scan to look for scarred brain tissue that can cause seizures. Even if the patient has not yet

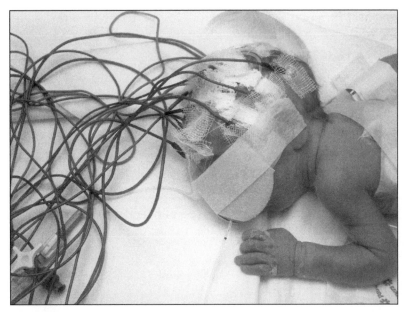

Brain-damaged babies with CP may undergo an EEG to determine whether additional problems are present.

had a seizure, the CAT scan can be useful in predicting whether one might occur in the future. The doctor may also order an electroencephalogram (EEG), which records electrical activity inside the brain. Combining the results of the CAT scan and EEG has proven to be a highly accurate means of predicting whether the patient will experience seizures. If the tests indicate that the patient might experience seizures in the future, the doctor instructs the patient's family members on what measures to take if a seizure does occur.

Checking Intelligence

Children who have been diagnosed with cerebral palsy are also often given an intelligence, or IQ, test to look for signs of mental retardation. Since many people with cerebral palsy cannot use their hands easily, this test is unlike commonly adminstered intelligence tests in which children have to use their hands to arrange blocks or puzzle pieces. Instead, the person giving the test moves the blocks or puzzle pieces for the child being tested and asks the child to indicate through speech or with a nod when the items being moved form a pattern. One mother of a cerebral palsy patient explains,

> The doctor suggested we take Zoe [her daughter] to a special psychologist who was experienced in giving IQ tests to children with cerebral palsy. Since I'm a teacher I know that many IQ tests for young children involve movement. Because Zoe has limited use of her hands and couldn't walk very well at the time, I was concerned that the test results might be invalid. But, she [the psychologist] gave Zoe a test that didn't require her to move about the room or use her hands. The test results were a relief. Her intelligence isn't affected. In fact, Zoe's IQ is above normal.[15]

Checking Vision

Finally, in order to check for vision problems, people with cerebral palsy are given vision tests. To check their visual sharpness, young patients, who cannot read, are asked to identify pictures from a distance of twenty feet. These pictures are of items commonly known to young children, such as a teddy bear or an apple. In addition,

Treatment for Cerebral Palsy

Treatment for cerebral palsy may include the following:

- Medication
- Braces
- Surgery
- Mechanical aids
- Counseling
- Physical therapy
- Occupational therapy
- Speech therapy
- Behavioral therapy

the way the child's eyes move is also examined. This helps the doctor diagnose weak eye muscles and crossed eyes.

Treatment Begins

Once any associated problems are diagnosed, treatment tailored to the type and severity of cerebral palsy begins. Treatment may include physical, occupational, and speech therapy; medication; special braces; and surgery.

The reason for the different treatment plans is that different types of cerebral palsy, and problems with different muscle groups, require different kinds of treatment. For example, if the muscles in the mouth, tongue, or vocal chords are involved, patients will eventually need speech therapy. Surgery to help relieve tight muscles in people with spastic cerebral palsy may also be prescribed. No matter what the treatment plan, though, the goal is to help patients control symptoms, improve their mobility, and enhance the quality of their lives.

Physical Therapy

Physical therapy is the most frequently prescribed treatment for cerebral palsy since it is effective in relieving symptoms of all types of the disorder. Physical therapy can help people with spastic cerebral palsy loosen tight muscles and become more flexible. It can improve the balance of people with ataxic cerebral palsy, and it can help people with athetoid cerebral palsy get more control over their muscles. During physical therapy patients are given an exercise program tailored to their needs.

In all cases, however, the goal is to help strengthen muscles and improve mobility. In daily physical therapy, specially trained physical therapists help patients develop the ability to stand, walk, run, negotiate stairs, or use a wheelchair. These physical therapy sessions may be held in hospitals or in separate physical therapy centers. These centers may resemble ordinary gyms; they are usually equipped with exercise mats, exercise bicycles, and weight training machines. But they are actually quite different because the staff are generally trained to provide for the individual needs of the clientele. Physical therapists also give families exercises to do at home with the patients as well as instruction on how to practice them safely. A physical therapist explains,

> Physical therapy [for cerebral palsy] places the focus on building muscle strength, coordination, balance and also managing the daily routine in learning new motor skills. Sessions typically take place in forty-five minute sessions, five times a week, and a continuous home program is important. Because of that, a physical therapist instructs a child's parents about safe and necessary home activities.[16]

Children with cerebral palsy often begin physical therapy treatment when they are as young as a year old, and it can be emotionally trying for parents to watch their youngsters go through exercises that are difficult or even painful. However, most people agree that the results are worth the effort. A woman whose son Jimmy has cerebral palsy and is being treated with physical therapy states,

> Jimmy was only sixteen months when he started therapy and from his first session he worked hard the entire hour. I watched Jimmy and his therapist. I watched how she held him, worked his muscles and seemed to control his movements. He was starting to use muscles in a way he never had before and some of it was painful. There are times when Jimmy cries, "Help me, Mom!" I want to grab him, run out the door and not come back. But I know that his therapist is not hurting him and he needs the therapy.[17]

Occupational Therapy

Like physical therapy, occupational therapy is effective for all types of cerebral palsy. Occupational therapy involves activities like stringing beads and creating art projects to help cerebral palsy patients develop or improve control of muscles in their hands, fingers, mouths, feet, and toes. Patients are also taught how to use muscles they can control in place of, or to assist, weaker ones. For example, patients who may not be able to use their hands to control their wheelchair may be taught how to

Occupational therapists fit a young CP patient with a physiotherapy chair and table. Therapy can help her to develop necessary skills.

control it with their feet or with a special device that they control by moving their head. One patient says, "I can drive my chair with my left foot, type and talk with my left knee. Of course, I have some nice people and equipment to help me."[18]

In addition, occupational therapists teach patients skills necessary for daily living. Many of these skills are difficult for someone whose movements are impaired. Patients learn how to dress, feed, groom, and bathe themselves as well as how to use the toilet without help, hold a pencil, manipulate a computer mouse, cut with scissors, write, and draw.

Occupational therapists also help people with cerebral palsy improve their ability to swallow. This is done through therapy in which patients are instructed in a variety of exercises and games. These involve tightening and relaxing the throat, moving the tongue in different positions, and keeping saliva in the mouth for timed intervals in order to strengthen weak muscles and teach patients new ways to swallow. A patient talks about how occupational therapy helped him:

When I was a little kid, I had a problem with drooling. My mouth would fill up with water. Instead of swallowing, I'd dribble all over myself. I couldn't control it, and it was really embarrassing. Other kids made fun of me. I started going to an occupational therapist and he taught me how to control the muscles in my mouth. That really helped with the drooling. Now, the only time I have trouble with drooling is when I get really excited.[19]

Speech Therapy

Since the goal is for most cerebral palsy patients to live as normally as possible, those whose symptoms include speech impairments often receive speech therapy. Speech therapists work to improve their clients' ability to produce the basic sounds that form words. By teaching patients how to position their tongues and mouths correctly, therapists help them speak more clearly. Therapy may also involve improving clients' ability to understand concepts and express themselves by expanding their vocabulary. One speech therapist explains the range of her activities:

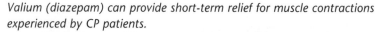

Valium (diazepam) can provide short-term relief for muscle contractions experienced by CP patients.

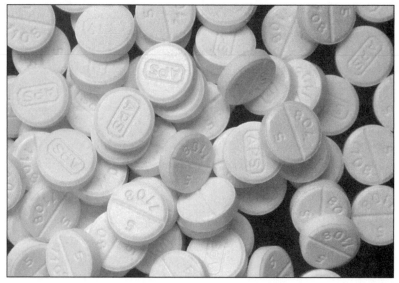

Speech therapy is aimed at helping people attain effective communication. As a speech therapist, I develop an individualized program for each of my clients that assists them to improve their understanding of language, and the clarity of their speech. Over the years, I've worked with a number of clients with cerebral palsy who were able to improve their vocal quality and speak more intelligibly. This raised their self-esteem, and improved the quality of their lives.[20]

Some people with cerebral palsy are unable to speak, however. When this is the case, speech therapists teach them to communicate in other ways. Some patients, for example, learn sign language. Patients who cannot use their hands well enough to use sign language learn to use special computers that communicate for them. For some patients, such devices are key to eliminating a sense of isolation. A patient explains,

> I went to Red Cross Elementary School for six and a half years. I had some hard times communicating with people in those years. I guess no one could understand me but my family. I didn't have many friends and that was ok. I only could say yes and no. Later I met a very great speech therapist. We started to work together. The first thing that we worked on was how to use the computer for communication.[21]

Medication

No amount of therapy, however, can repair the damaged brain cells that underlie cerebral palsy, nor are there drugs that accomplish this. However, there are some medications that can help lessen the severity of a patient's symptoms. For example, doctors sometimes prescribe a drug called diazepam, or Valium, which can help control some of the unwanted muscle contractions that are part of spastic cerebral palsy. Under the influence of diazepam, tight spastic muscles loosen. Diazepam gives patients only short-term relief, however. The drug does not appear to have any long-term value in controlling spastic muscles. Once diazepam leaves the body, patients' muscles tighten again. Diazepam can also trigger side effects such as drowsiness, and long-term use can result in addiction. For this reason, diazepam is used only for short periods.

Whereas diazepam can help those with spastic cerebral palsy, other medications, known as anticholinergic drugs, sometimes provide relief for people with athetoid cerebral palsy. These drugs, of which the most common are benztropine and trihexyphenidyl, reduce involuntary muscle movement. The response of patients to these drugs is unpredictable, however. Although anticholinergic drugs help some people with athetoid cerebral palsy, these drugs increase involuntary muscle movements in others. Doctors are not sure why this happens. For this reason, patients taking anticholinergic drugs must be closely monitored.

Doctors also prescribe drugs known as anticonvulsants for people with cerebral palsy who have seizures. The selection of anticonvulsants is wide and includes phenobarbital, zarontin, tegretol, and klonopin. These drugs control seizures by slowing the movement of abnormal electrical activity in the brain. This reduces the number of seizures people have.

Depending on the frequency and severity of their seizures, some patients may take more than one of these drugs. As one parent states,

> Like many children with cerebral palsy, Zoe [her daughter] had severe seizures. Sometimes she would have three or four seizures in a day. When she started on tegretol she went down to two or three seizures a week. Now, she takes both tegretol and klonopin, and she's down to about one seizure a month. It's a lot of medication for her to take, but we're really excited about the results.[22]

Braces

The side effects of medication are often undesirable; the drugs can cause dizziness, drowsiness, nausea, and other problems. So some patients choose to use mechanical devices to help control their symptoms. Among the most common devices are special braces that are used to help stretch and loosen tight muscles or provide support and strengthen weak muscles. Braces also help reset awkwardly bent muscles into more useful positions. Made of lightweight plastic, braces are worn over a patient's foot, ankle, leg, hip, or hand, depending on what muscles are being treated. Orthotists, the people who make such devices, custom-mold each patient's braces in order to guarantee a perfect fit. As patients grow and the size and shape of their muscles change, the braces must be replaced.

The process of constructing custom-made braces is exact and time-consuming. Measuring can be difficult. The patient must be perfectly still for the measurement to be correct. This can be especially difficult for patients with athetoid cerebral palsy, whose muscles move involuntarily.

Still, for most patients, the experience is not unpleasant. It usually takes about two weeks for the braces to be ready. A mother describes her son's experience:

> We went into a little room and I took Jimmy's shoes off and rolled up his pants. The orthotist was warm and friendly. He sang a children's song while he rolled the wet plaster on Jimmy's legs. I had to hold Jimmy down and try to soothe him at the same time. We left after the fitting and scheduled a time to pick up Jimmy's new "shoes" [foot braces].[23]

Once braces are fitted and made, people with cerebral palsy wear them all day. Some people sleep in them, too. Although braces are made to fit comfortably, most people need to get used to wearing them. At first they can feel quite cumbersome. In addition, hip and long leg braces can make sitting difficult.

Despite these problems, after a few months the braces feel more natural. By wrapping securely around affected limbs, braces allow patients to use the limbs more easily. For example, a foot brace provides support for foot and ankle muscles that are weak from disuse. With the help of a foot brace, patients who previously had little choice but to sit in a wheelchair can stand more easily. Moreover, once patients are standing, they are using their foot and ankle muscles more, which helps the muscles to grow and become stronger. The brace also puts tension on the muscle. This loosens, lengthens, and straightens tight, contracted muscles, at the same time repositioning them in ways that make movement easier. A mother describes the effect of braces on her daughter: "My daughter, now fifteen months, and not walking yet, has been wearing an AFO [ankle-fitting orthotonic] for about six weeks now. We have noticed improvement in her strength and balance. I think mostly because all she wants to do is walk all over holding our fingers. The AFO has helped her hold her foot flat in the correct position."[24] This family's experience has been supported by research. For example, a study in Somerset Hospital in England monitored the effectiveness of ankle braces on children whose cerebral palsy left them with spastic ankle and foot muscles. The study found that the braces enabled the children to gain mobility, and at the same time they lengthened tight, contracted muscles in their ankles. This delayed the need for surgery in these muscles in all of the children who were tested.

Surgery

Although braces do help stretch contracted muscles and reduce tightness, sometimes spastic muscles are so stiff and bent only surgery can provide relief. One of the more commonly performed operations is aimed at lengthening the Achilles tendon. Done under general anesthesia, this surgery involves doctors making a large cut behind the patient's ankle and stretching the tendon.

Because this is major surgery, the recovery is long and uncomfortable. After surgery, patients wear a cast from their toes to their knee that keeps the tendon in place. Usually the cast has a sole on the bottom, which allows patients to stand and walk on it immediately. Patients usually wear the cast for about six weeks. When the cast comes off, patients often follow a special physical therapy program that further stretches their Achilles tendon in an effort to keep the tendon from contracting again. In 25 percent of all cases, however, the physical therapy is unsuccessful and the tendon does contract again. When this happens the surgery must be redone. In fact, patients sometimes have this surgery three or four times. Similar surgeries can also be performed on contracted elbows, fingers, thumbs, shoulders, wrists, thighs, hamstrings, and hip muscles.

Supportive braces benefit people with CP by loosening and strengthening tight muscles.

These types of surgeries offer patients many benefits. They give people with cerebral palsy increased use of the muscles and improve patients' ability to move around. In some cases, surgery can even help patients who were unable to walk to start walking. Of course, these procedures are all major surgeries and carry with them certain risks, such as adverse reactions to anesthesia and postoperative complications like bleeding and infection. But many patients choose surgery anyway because the result of an operation can be a dramatic improvement in one's mobility.

No treatment, including surgery, can cure cerebral palsy. However, all treatments for cerebral palsy can improve patients' muscle development and control. This improves their ability to move and the quality of their lives.

Chapter 3

Alternative Treatments

E VEN WHEN PEOPLE with cerebral palsy follow an individualized treatment plan, they still may not achieve the level of muscle control and ease of movement that they desire. Consequently, many people with cerebral palsy combine alternative treatments with conventional ones. Although experts question the value of some of these treatments, others are gradually gaining wider recognition as being effective in relieving some symptoms of cerebral palsy. Those who receive such treatments often speak enthusiastically of the results, despite the discomfort they may experience. A young man with cerebral palsy talks about the alternative treatment he has participated in:

> If I knew someone with cerebral palsy, I would tell them to speak to my mom and dad, who know a lot about medicine and doctors. They found out about alternative medicine. When I was two years old, I went to Anat [an alternative practitioner]. She did exercises with me that I didn't like. The positions she put me in hurt. I was too little to know that the exercises were going to help me. Dr. Fryman [another alternative practitioner] makes me more relaxed and loosens my body. None of this makes my disability go away. But it makes it easier to live with.[25]

Controversial Therapy

As the name implies, alternative treatment is one that is not widely accepted by mainstream medical practitioners in the United States and Europe. One reason for this is that, unlike conventional treatments, which are subjected to rigorous testing before being approved by regulatory agencies such as the Food and Drug Administration, many alternative treatments undergo only limited testing and evidence of their effectiveness is mostly anecdotal— that is, it includes primarily individual stories from patients on how the treatment worked for them. In addition, studies of alternative treatments do not usually compare their results to those of a control group that receives conventional treatment. And the number of patients participating in these studies is usually not large enough to be scientifically sound. For these reasons, those who wish to try alternative treatments must decide whether the potential benefits outweigh the risks of wasting time, effort, and money and of suffering severe side effects.

Despite these concerns, many health care professionals believe that a combination of alternative and conventional treatments, known as complementary treatment, can be effective in relieving symptoms of cerebral palsy. Many doctors and other health care professionals agree that complementary treatment can help reduce pain, relax and loosen stiff muscles, improve balance, and teach patients ways to better control involuntary movement. According to cerebral palsy expert Andrew Vickers, "Complementary medicine is not a cure for cerebral palsy. Cerebral palsy cannot be cured by complementary or any other form of medicine, simply because cerebral palsy involves damage to the nervous system. This cannot be reversed. But complementary therapies do sometimes lead to significant improvements."[26]

Three Types of Treatment

Despite the controversy over their effectiveness, alternative treatments for cerebral palsy are often tried, particularly when more conventional therapy fails to bring relief of symptoms. Although the specific treatment regimens vary widely, they fall into three categories: hands-on treatments, mechanical treatments, and indirect treatments. Of these, hands-on treatments are the most frequently used. Hands-on treatments are widely believed to loosen stiff muscles, in the process enabling people with cerebral palsy to become more mobile. Within this broad category, options vary widely, but three—chiropractic treatment, cranial manipulation, and acupressure—are the most widely practiced.

Chiropractic Treatment

Among the options open to cerebral palsy patients, chiropractic treatment is one of the most common. It involves the external manipulation or adjustment of the spine in order to relieve pressure on nerves. Chiropractors believe that since 95 percent of the body's nerve impulses travel from the brain through the spinal cord, the body's ability to function is affected by what happens in and around the spine. Problems arise when contorted muscles caused by cerebral palsy put pressure on spinal nerves, causing them to become blocked and keeping electrical impulses from moving freely from the brain to the muscles. This makes it difficult for people with cerebral palsy to control their muscles. Therefore, by massaging and applying mild force to the spine, chiropractors relieve pressure on the nerves, allowing messages from the brain to reach the muscles.

Chiropractic, a common treatment for CP patients, involves manipulating the spine.

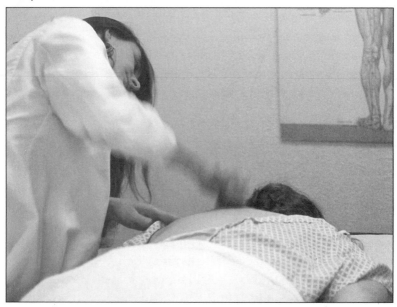

This type of treatment is so popular because many cerebral palsy patients credit chiropractic manipulation with helping them develop more control over their muscles and allowing them greater mobility.

Many mainstream cerebral palsy researchers are skeptical of chiropractic treatment. Those researchers do not believe that manipulating a patient's spine can have any effect on his or her muscles. However, chiropractic therapy has become so popular that the National Institutes of Health is currently studying its effects on the spinal cord.

A patient who believes chiropractic treatment has helped her manage her cerebral palsy talks about her experience:

> I want everyone to know how much chiropractic care has improved my ability to manage my CP [cerebral palsy]. I am twenty-four years old and have been receiving chiropractic care for one year. When I first started, I had not walked in three years. I could not stand up straight, and my legs felt like lead. My knees hurt, and I was unable to relax my muscles. There were times when my head would fall backwards—I had no control over it. I now walk on a daily basis—either unassisted or with the use of crutches. I can stand up straight and my legs feel lighter. I can maintain balance while walking, and walk at a faster pace. My contractures [muscle tightness] are starting to release a little more. My brain and feet are starting to communicate more. My only regret is that I wish I had found out about this sooner.[27]

Cranial Manipulation

Somewhat more controversial than chiropractic treatment is cranial manipulation, a treatment that is based on the theory that bones in the skull are not inflexible and can be shifted. Changes in the bones' arrangement, some practitioners claim, can affect the brain and the way it communicates with the rest of the body. Administered by specialists known as cranial osteopaths, cranial manipulation involves applying mild pressure to the head and neck. This action promotes the release of cerebrospinal fluid, a

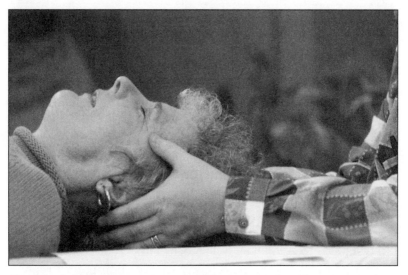

Cranial manipulation, a controversial CP treatment, is said to promote the release of a fluid that lubricates the brain and spinal cord.

fluid that lubricates the brain and spinal cord. When cerebrospinal fluid is released, cranial osteopaths say it makes it easier for nerve impulses from the brain to reach the muscles.

This theory has not yet been proven and many experts consider cranial manipulation ineffective. However, many people with cerebral palsy say they have found cranial manipulation to be beneficial. Laura Shapiro Kramer, a cerebral palsy expert and the mother of a child with the disorder, explains, "Physicians who are trained in craniosacral therapy [cranial manipulation] use their techniques to identify all kinds of disturbed patterns of movement, to treat and diagnose many disorders in a gentle, noninvasive way, and the effects of this treatment can be far reaching."[28]

Acupressure

Cranial manipulation purportedly achieves its results by clearing barriers to nerve impulses. Somewhat less understandable, at least to Western-trained practitioners, is the idea underlying another popular hands-on treatment for cerebral palsy, acupressure. Acupressure is an ancient form of Chinese medicine based on the theory that healthy people have a life-energy called *chi* flowing through their bodies; if this energy becomes blocked, illness and pain occur. To relieve these blockages, acupressurists apply pressure to specific points in the body to stimulate their flow of energy. This makes it easier for nerve impulses from the brain to travel throughout the body and allows improved blood supply to reach undamaged brain cells. When more blood reaches the brain, acupressurists say, the brain cells controlling muscles are strengthened and other undamaged brain cells take over some of the functions previously assigned to damaged brain cells. As a result, tight muscles relax and patients gain greater muscle control.

There is little evidence in Western science to prove that these energy channels exist, and many Western practitioners are skeptical of the treatment's benefits. However, acupressure has been widely studied in China, and these studies indicate that acupressure can improve the ability of people with cerebral palsy to control their muscles and their mobility. Certainly, the anecdotal evidence is

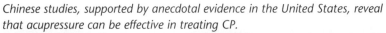

Chinese studies, supported by anecdotal evidence in the United States, reveal that acupressure can be effective in treating CP.

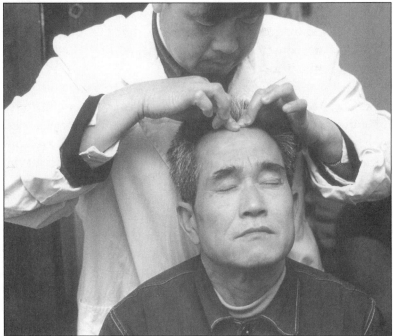

encouraging. A Chinese doctor and acupressurist who works at the Institute of Orthopedics and Traumatology in Bejing describes the effect of acupressure on one of his patients:

> When six year old Tan was first taken to the outpatient department of the Institute, she could not even grasp chopsticks or a pen. When she walked her right heel was suspended in the air. After 120 treatments [with acupressure], Tan could write with a pen and her gait became normal while walking slowly. Only when she walked fast or ran, did she show slight signs of limping.[29]

Mechanical Treatments

Just as acupressure has many loyal adherents, so too do mechanical treatments. As the name suggests, these are administered through the use of mechanical devices rather than by human hands. Electrical stimulation and biofeedback are two forms of mechanical treatments.

Electrical stimulation involves the use of very low levels of electricity to stimulate tight muscles and help them to relax. Electrical stimulation's proponents say that this treatment replaces the nervous impulses that damaged brain cells would otherwise generate.

Electrical stimulation is usually used to help those with spastic cerebral palsy walk. It involves the placement of electrodes on both sides of a patient's leg, below the knee. These electrodes, which are stuck to the skin with double-sided tape, are connected to a small power source called a stimulator. About the size of a deck of cards, the stimulator is placed in the patient's pocket or belt. It is also connected to a switch that is worn in the patient's shoe. When the patient puts weight on the foot, the switch is pressed, activating the stimulator to send electrical impulses through the electrodes to the muscles in the lower leg. The muscles then relax, allowing the patient to pick up his or her foot and move it. As the foot is picked up, the muscle contracts again. This alternating relaxation and contraction mimics, to some extent, the action of normal muscles.

Research on the use of electrical stimulation is somewhat better documented than studies of other alternative therapies and suggests that it does allow people with cerebral palsy to walk faster with less effort. In one study conducted in England in 1995, sixteen subjects with spastic cerebral palsy were treated with physical therapy and electrical stimulation; sixteen subjects were also treated with physical therapy alone. The walking speed and muscle tightness of both groups were measured weekly. At the close of the study, the subjects treated with physical therapy and electrical stimulation improved the most. Their walking speed increased by 16 percent, and their muscle tightness decreased significantly. This was not the case in the control group; these patients' walking speed increased by only about 5 percent. Based on this and other studies, many doctors endorse the use of electrical stimulation as a complement to standard treatment for cerebral palsy.

Biofeedback

Another alternative therapy that is gradually gaining the respect of mainstream doctors is biofeedback. This therapy involves teaching patients how to monitor and then gradually control previously involuntary body functions, such as heart rate and muscle tension. Biofeedback has been reported to help patients learn how to relax tight muscles, control involuntary muscle movement, and treat seizures.

Biofeedback treatment involves attaching sensors to the patient's forehead and connecting these to monitors that measure activity in patients' brains and muscles. A computer then translates the brain activity or muscle movement into a light or sound patients can see or hear. For example, when patients tense a muscle, a picture appears on a computer screen, a light flashes, or a bell rings. In this manner, people are able to see or hear tangible evidence of the muscles their cerebral palsy has impaired. The goal, then, is for the patient to slow down the flashing or ringing or change the picture on the computer screen by thinking about relaxing the muscle in question. In the same way, patients with athetoid or ataxic cerebral palsy can learn to control involuntary muscle movement.

Another benefit of biofeedback is that it can help people with cerebral palsy become aware of the signs that a seizure is about to occur. With practice, some people learn to master the misfiring of nerve impulses that causes seizures. A patient explains, "Biofeedback has enabled me to actually keep my seizures under control. Whenever I feel an aura [abnormal electrical surge in the brain] coming on, I am able to stop it from fully progressing into a seizure."[30]

Although research into the effects of biofeedback on people with cerebral palsy is limited, results of studies that have been conducted are promising. According to the Association for Applied Psychophysiology and Biofeedback, "Researchers proved that many individuals could alter their involuntary responses by being fed back information about what was occurring in their bodies. As a result, biofeedback can train individuals with techniques for living a healthier life."[31] Biofeedback equipment is quite expensive, though, and treatment costs are more than many people can afford. Thus, although use of biofeedback is increasing, few people actually have access to this technology.

Indirect Treatments

Hands-on and mechanical treatments require specially trained therapists, specialized and often expensive equipment, or both. Indirect treatments, however, emphasize activities and exercises that build muscle strength and control in ways that allow for somewhat greater independence. Popular indirect treatments for cerebral palsy include yoga, swimming, and therapeutic horseback riding.

Yoga

Yoga is a form of exercise that originated in ancient India and involves slow, controlled stretching while the body is held in certain postures. The combination of stretching and posture work relaxes the body and stretches and loosens tight muscles. Over time, practicing yoga also stretches and straightens the spine. When the spine is stretched, there is less pressure on nerves radiating from the spine. Yoga adherents say this makes it easier for nerve impulses to travel from the brain to the muscles. For

Yet another nontraditional treatment regimen, yoga, has proved helpful for people suffering from CP.

people with cerebral palsy, this translates into control over muscles and movement.

A number of studies have found that yoga benefits people with a wide range of disabilities, including cerebral palsy. Benefits are so widely accepted that yoga classes are offered in many hospitals, and special classes at health clubs and yoga studios are often offered for people with disabilities. A mother of a child with cerebral palsy describes the effect of yoga on her son:

> The effect on his body tone was immediately noticeable. His sitting posture and sitting balance improved. His body tone, especially in the shoulders, arms, and hands relaxed, enabling

him to more easily perform tasks. His head and neck alignment improved, allowing him to hold his head erect for significantly longer periods of time. Because of the benefits of regular practice [of yoga] it became apparent to his physician and therapist that, due to decreased muscle tone [looser, more relaxed muscles], surgery was no longer necessary.[32]

Swimming

Swimming or exercising in water also offers many benefits. Such exercise helps strengthen, stretch, and loosen tight muscles, and swimming gives people with cerebral palsy a feeling of freedom. Many people with cerebral palsy cannot move about without the aid of a wheelchair or crutches, but in a swimming pool the buoyancy of water allows them to move freely. One cerebral palsy patient states, "I move awkwardly on land, but I'm faster and more graceful than a lot of people in the water. Swimming makes me feel strong."[33]

Swimming exercises offer a CP patient the welcome sensations of mobility and freedom.

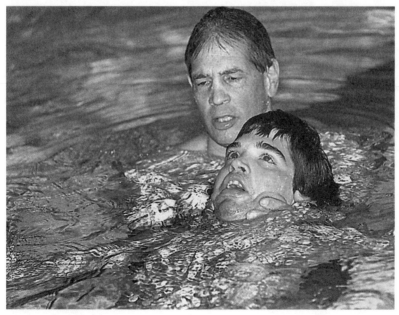

Swimming has been found to be so beneficial for people with cerebral palsy that many doctors recommend it. As a result, many people with cerebral palsy attend special swimming and water exercise classes for people with disabilities or receive private lessons. Instruction is usually given in a special therapy pool where the water temperature is kept at about ninety-two degrees. This is because warm water relaxes the body and stiff muscles.

Therapeutic Horseback Riding

Better even than swimming as a means of building strength and increasing flexibility is therapeutic horseback riding, or hippotherapy. In this type of therapy, people with cerebral palsy are supervised by specially trained instructors and carefully taught how to ride. At first, special ropes and props may be used to keep the rider in an upright position while the instructor walks beside the horse in order to prevent falls. With time, though, riders usually are able to ride without the help of the instructor.

Research has shown that therapeutic horseback riding is beneficial for several reasons. It loosens tight leg and arm muscles, promotes good posture, and increases balance and muscle strength. Since maintaining balance on a moving horse requires the rider to use many muscles, people with cerebral palsy strengthen all the muscles involved in sitting.

In addition, therapeutic horseback riding has been shown to improve speech in people with cerebral palsy. Many people with cerebral palsy who have speech disabilities may be reluctant to speak because they are often misunderstood. However, a rider must vocalize in order to communicate with the horse. With practice, the cerebral palsy patient's speech gains clarity, and he or she develops more confidence in speaking.

Therapeutic horseback riding not only helps people with cerebral palsy develop physically, but it also raises patients' self-esteem. As the individual gains control over the horse, he or she tends to feel increasingly empowered. A mother whose son Seth was treated with therapeutic horseback riding for cerebral palsy describes how it benefited her son:

Seth loved being on horseback. His instructor demanded that he sit properly on the horse, keep himself erect, and push his heels down so his hip flexors [muscles] stretched. I could see his head come into alignment and his carriage [posture] improve. Seth's relationship with the horses, such big animals, encouraged him to think of himself as powerful. Riding was good for his self-esteem.[34]

A Controversial Treatment

Alternative treatments such as hippotherapy, swimming, and yoga are gradually gaining a measure of acceptance as anecdotal evidence of their effectiveness grows. But the effectiveness and even the safety of other treatments, which have not been tested or used widely, are open to question. For example, a regimen known as hyperbaric oxygen treatment, based on the theory that supplying the brain with large doses of oxygen can repair the brain damage caused by oxygen deprivations, is being touted by some therapists. The treatment involves placing patients in special pressurized chambers in which they are given pure oxygen. However, no research has indicated that hyperbaric oxygen treatment is effective in helping ease symptoms in people with cerebral palsy. And many doctors believe that arguments to the contrary lack merit. Researcher and cerebral palsy expert Dr. Peter Rosenbaum scoffs at the idea of using hyperbaric chambers to treat cerebral palsy: "The logic that we can repair brain impairment caused by oxygen deprivation by supplying more oxygen after the damage has been done is just crazy. The underlying brain damage is permanent, and neither improves or worsens."[35]

The Risks of Alternative Treatments

Although many patients are turning to alternative treatments hoping to develop better muscle control and improve their mobility, these treatments, like conventional ones, can pose health risks. One of the greatest risks occurs when people replace conventional treatments that have been proven to work with alternative treatments of unproven or little value. Moreover, although alternative treatments may improve muscle control in patients,

A young CP patient's face shines with delight during a hippotherapy session.

they tend to be geared toward increasing control over individual muscles rather than emphasizing the goal of enhancing overall mobility. In this way, the individual who bypasses conventional treatment in favor of even the most effective alternative therapies reduces his or her chances of becoming mobile.

A lack of regulations and standards for licensing many practitioners of alternative therapies also exposes patients to real health hazards. For example, there have been cases in which inadequately trained practitioners placed electrodes for electrical stimulation over broken skin, rashes, or blisters, causing serious skin irritation. Problems also have been reported when alternative practitioners who are not trained or experienced in working with people with cerebral palsy apply too much pressure to weak muscles. This overstimulates the muscles, causing muscle spasms, muscle tears, and other serious injuries.

The best results appear to occur when people with cerebral palsy combine alternative and conventional treatments. Such a combination can increase the patient's muscle control and mobility, decrease seizures, and improve speech. The overall effect is an improved quality of life. According to a patient who successfully combines alternative and conventional treatment, "I take medication for seizures, work with a physical therapist, swim, and do yoga. I know none of this will cure me. But it makes me feel stronger and happier."[36]

Chapter 4

Living with Cerebral Palsy

THERE IS NO known cure for cerebral palsy. For those who have the disorder and for their families, the goal becomes learning how to live with cerebral palsy. Having a severe disability impacts every aspect of life, yet with the help of special equipment and a caring support network, people with cerebral palsy can lead happy, productive, and independent lives. A patient talks about her life:

> I am nineteen years old and a senior in high school. I have CP and get around in a motorized wheelchair that I call "The Bomb." I'm lucky to have a great family and good friends who look out for me. But being a teenager with CP is no party. There are lots of things I'd kill to be able to do, like dance and walk around the mall on my own two feet. But I don't let CP get me down. I figure everyone faces challenges in life and CP is my challenge.[37]

Limited Mobility

Among the biggest challenges people with cerebral palsy face are the barriers to movement that are an unintended part of virtually every structure. Doorways, particularly in older homes, are often too narrow to accommodate wheelchairs, for example. Even a single step, not to mention an entire flight of stairs, can be an insurmountable barrier for people with limited use of their legs. An article in the *Denver Post* explains how this problem affected Katrina Chapman, a teenager with cerebral palsy. According to

Chapman's mother, "We had two portable, aluminum ramps that I would set outside [over a flight of stairs] each morning and each afternoon when Katrina would come home from school. . . . Sometimes they wouldn't be level or the ground would be icy and her wheelchair would tilt over."[38]

However, sometimes small, relatively inexpensive modifications can greatly improve a person's ability to get around. Wheelchair ramps and handrails in hallways can be quite helpful. And changes, such as replacing hard-to-turn doorknobs with easier lever-style door handles can make the difference between independence and dependence. A patient whose home was remodeled to accommodate her impairments explains, "I guess I didn't think about how limited I was before, but I can do a lot of things on my own now that I wasn't able to do before."[39]

A youth at a CP center uses a lift to board a school bus. More modest modifications can also help CP patients overcome physical barriers.

Challenges in Public Areas

Similar access problems arise in public areas. Despite the Americans with Disabilities Act (ADA), a federal law that requires that public places built after 1990 be accessible to people with disabilities, aisles in older stores are often too cluttered or narrow to allow access by people in wheelchairs. Even in modern shopping malls that were built to comply with the ADA, fast-moving crowds present difficulties for people with cerebral palsy since their limited mobility and difficulties with balance leave them vulnerable to being pushed over or knocked down. A young woman with cerebral palsy notes that sometimes the difficulties make going to her local mall not worth the trouble:

> I love clothes, and I love to shop. But I can't go to lots of small stores because the aisles are too narrow for my wheelchair. I can't depend on using one of those electric scooters that the big stores are supposed to provide, because lots of stores have only one or two, and half the time they're broken. Shopping can be a real problem for a fashion lover like me. So, I've started shopping on the Internet instead.[40]

Transportation can also be a problem for people with limited mobility. Entering and exiting taxis, cars, buses, and subways can be troublesome. Driving can also be difficult for cerebral palsy patients who do not have use of their legs. To help make transportation more accessible, the ADA requires cities to provide special buses equipped with hydraulic lifts that make it possible for people in wheelchairs to board them. In addition, cars can be outfitted with special adaptive devices that allow people with cerebral palsy to drive without the use of their legs. This can be quite expensive, but there are organizations, such as the United Cerebral Palsy Association (UCPA), that can link people who need money to donors who help pay for these special cars.

Challenges in School

School presents a special challenge for people with cerebral palsy. Such students may have difficulty, for example, sitting in the kind of chairs with which classrooms are furnished. And moving from class to class can be a time-consuming process, particularly when the school building is multifloored or the campus is large. But when students work together with their school to arrange modifications, such as gaining access to more accommodating chairs, use of an elevator, or being assigned a special aide to help them maneuver crowded halls, these challenges can be met.

The challenges presented by the physical environment of schools are only the beginning for many students with cerebral palsy. For instance, students may have difficulty raising their hands, taking notes, and carrying heavy books. For this reason, many students with cerebral palsy attend special-education classes with other physically challenged students for part of the day. In this environment, specially trained teachers give students academic support in classrooms that are supplied with special equipment designed to accommodate their physical impairments. At the same time, speech therapists work on improving their speech problems.

Students often spend the rest of the day in regular classrooms with physically able students in a process known as mainstreaming. This provides them with the opportunity to interact with both physically challenged and able students. A young woman with cerebral palsy says, "I attend academic classes in the resource room [special-education classroom] for part of the day, but I'm mainstreamed for art, music, and computer ed. Mainstreaming can be tough. The classes move quickly, and sometimes, I'm still trying to raise my hand after the question has been answered. But mainstreaming is preparing me for surviving in the real world because the real world moves fast too."[41]

Speech Problems

Speech problems present another challenge for people with cerebral palsy. Being unable to communicate effectively makes daily living difficult and can be emotionally challenging. It can be very frustrating for a person to be unable to communicate his or her thoughts and feelings to others. Furthermore, misunderstandings often occur. A newspaper article in the *Australian* describes a cerebral palsy patient's experience: "In the hospital to have her

Speech difficulties often frustrate people with CP. Special computers can translate a CP patient's speech, enhancing communication.

appendix removed, she called for a nurse to adjust her bed so she could go to sleep. Hearing her cries but not understanding her, the nurse instead gave her an enema, assuming she was in pain."[42]

Moreover, since many people with cerebral palsy speak slowly and unclearly, people frequently misjudge them, believing that their slow or unclear response is due to lack of intelligence. This can lower patients' self-esteem and self-confidence. However, by using special computers that help make communication easier, people with cerebral palsy meet this challenge. For example, computers can be equipped with speech synthesizers that translate words into intelligible sounds. Although the earliest synthesizers produced a mechanical-sounding voice, advances in software have meant that new synthesizers can produce a voice that is virtually indistinguishable from human speech. The software even offers the option of a male or female voice.

Head Pointers

The computers that provide a voice for people with cerebral palsy can even be used by those who have little or no use of their hands. These patients use an attachment, called a head pointer, to make their computers work. A head pointer allows people to type on a computer keyboard, write, and even paint with their head by attaching a paint brush to the head pointer. Most head pointers look like a helmet with a long pointing stick attached. The helmet is held on with adjustable elastic straps that fit around a person's forehead and jaw. A pointer is attached to the forehead strap. When wearers move their head, the pointer also moves. (Some head pointers require even less head movement and have pointers extending out from the wearer's jaw instead of the forehead.)

Head pointers have proved very popular with cerebral palsy patients because they provide a sense of connection to the outside world the patients lack otherwise. Artist Dan Keplinger, who uses a head pointer, explains how being able to paint has improved his life: "Once I discovered art, I no longer felt disabled. I had an identity. With painting I could express myself clearly without anybody interpreting for me. People think I don't have any thoughts or emotions. It's a frustration that never goes away. . . . The world could now hear I was a person."[43]

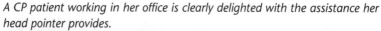

A CP patient working in her office is clearly delighted with the assistance her head pointer provides.

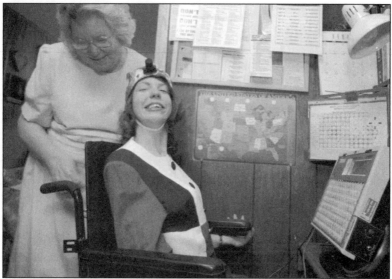

Feeling Excluded

Other emotional issues arise when, because of their disabilities, people with cerebral palsy are treated differently by their peers. For example, people with cerebral palsy often find themselves excluded from social activities attended by their able-bodied peers. Moreover, young people with cerebral palsy are often teased or picked on by ignorant classmates. A young man with cerebral palsy recalls,

> I didn't have many friends when I was little. The other kids either ignored me or made fun of me. The first time was in kindergarten when the other kids made fun of me because of the way I walked. That really hurt. I didn't choose to walk this way. Even the nicer kids didn't think about inviting me to their birthday parties or sleepovers. What some people don't realize is that I'm a person, even if I have a disability.[44]

Finding Support

One way people with cerebral palsy meet the challenge of feeling excluded is by joining a support group consisting of others with cerebral palsy. In this way, members get a chance to share their feelings with those who are likely to empathize while providing information and encouragement to others. By sharing their common experiences, support-group members are able to work toward solutions to problems that people without cerebral palsy have difficulty comprehending.

A patient who is a member of one such group explains how it has helped her:

> I've made lots of good friends in the group. Our friendship is based on who we are, not on our appearance. We don't judge each other. It doesn't matter if someone can walk or not. We're there for each other. We provide each other with support and understanding that our friends without CP can't provide. We share our problems and inspire each other with our successes. Being in touch with people with CP who are living independently and doing for themselves makes me confident that I can do it too.[45]

In addition, many groups partner with health care professionals and cerebral palsy organizations to provide patients with current information on every aspect of the disorder. Organizations such as the UCPA, for example, sponsor local support groups all over the United States. And there are electronic support groups that share information via the Internet. These groups offer information on many topics, including treatment options and new medicines and assistive devices.

Summer Camp

Support groups are often designed for cerebral palsy patients of all ages. For children and teens, however, there is yet another opportunity to gather with those who share the disability: summer camp. Sponsored by groups like the United Cerebral Palsy Association, cerebral palsy camps give juveniles with the disorder a chance to make new friends and to participate in physical activities, including horseback riding, fishing, swimming, and boating, that accommodate their limitations and strengthen their muscles. Each camper is assigned a personal volunteer who provides them with assistance and keeps them safe. All the while, campers are having fun with young people like themselves.

Research has shown that attending summer camp helps young people with cerebral palsy to develop physical and social skills, which in turn helps them meet the challenge of daily living. According to the UCPA, "For special needs children, camping improves both their self-confidence and self-reliance; builds a can-do sense among campers who achieve goals among others with similar disabilities, promotes emotional development and maturity; and helps to develop a sense of personal capability."[46]

Staying Active

Although summer camps are designed for youngsters, people with cerebral palsy find that no matter what their age, participating in recreational activities helps them develop a sense of confidence in their personal capability. Such participation allows people with cerebral palsy to strengthen their mind and body while having fun and making new friends. For example, special trips to museums

In a stunning achievement, a young CP patient plays soccer with nondisabled teammates.

and movies sponsored by organizations like the UCPA and visits by guest lecturers help people to grow intellectually.

Participation in athletic activities, in particular, challenges people with cerebral palsy to reach their full potential physically and, in so doing, increases their self-esteem. Sports organizations for those with disabilities, such as the International Paralympic Committee and the Cerebral Palsy Sports and Recreation Association, exist all over the world and offer special sports programs for athletes who are physically challenged. Typical programs include wheelchair basketball, wheelchair racing, bicycle racing, track and field, and swimming.

For people who prefer noncompetitive activities, other sports and activities are available. The National Sports Center for the Disabled provides information on campgrounds and ski areas that are accessible to physically challenged people. The **Therapeutic Golf Foundation teaches people with cerebral palsy how to play golf, and local** chapters of the United Cerebral Palsy Association offer special recreational programs. These include swimming, arts and crafts, field trips, tai chi, wheelchair basketball, and many other activities. In addition, most Boy Scout and Girl Scout troops welcome disabled members.

Participation in any of these activities helps people with cerebral palsy to connect with the world around them, improving the quality of their lives in the process. A young woman with cerebral palsy explains, "I was involved in Girl Scouts for ten years. It gave me a chance to do lots of things. My favorite was volunteering at a nursing home. That made me realize that there are people way worse off than me, and that I could help them. I learned lots of things through Girl Scouts, especially how capable I actually am."[47]

Feeling Dependent

Feeling excluded is not the only emotional challenge people with cerebral palsy face, they frequently must depend on others to assist them with simple activities that most people can do independently. These activities may include dressing, bathing, cutting food, writing, and standing. This can be frustrating. According to a young woman with cerebral palsy,

> I sometimes want to scream when I can't do something. I often have to wait for people to do things for me, like take me to the bathroom, dress me, get me a drink, or even turn over a tape in the tape recorder. The easiest way to deal with this

A service dog can liberate a CP patient from a life of stifling dependency.

dependency is to ask for what I need and then be infinitely patient while I wait. But the companion of that patience is often hidden frustration.[48]

Service Dogs

Having a service dog is one way people with cerebral palsy cope with the frustration of feeling dependent. Service dogs are specially trained to help those with a wide range of physical disabilities to live more independently. Service dogs can pull manual wheelchairs, help people keep their balance, and pull people up when they have fallen. They can carry items in their mouths and retrieve items their owners may have dropped. Moreover, some service dogs are trained to help people get dressed, open and close doors by pulling a rope attached to the doorknob, turn light switches on and off, press elevator buttons, bring the phone when it rings, wear a backpack filled with their owners' supplies, and bark for help when necessary. Besides being tireless helpers, service dogs provide their owners with companionship.

Service dogs are trained as part of special programs sponsored by groups such as the Canine Companions for Independence, Paws for a Cause, and Assistance Dogs International. Each service dog is trained especially for a specific individual. Because of their intelligence and helpful nature, most service dogs are Labrador retrievers, German shepherds, or a mix of these breeds.

Would-be service dogs are usually trained for their role from the time they are puppies, around four months of age. After about a year of training in the skills needed to be a good service dog, the animal undergoes two to three weeks of additional intensive training with its new owner. This gives the owner a chance to learn how to command the dog and allows the dog and its owner to bond with each other. It costs about twenty thousand dollars to breed, raise, and train one service dog. However, these costs are covered by charitable donations, and service dogs are provided free to people who need them.

Having a service dog can change the life of a person with cerebral palsy for the better, giving them newfound freedom and independence. As one patient states:

I was born with spastic diplegic cerebral palsy. For twenty-three years, I have tried to become independent. In September of 1996, a friend told me about Paws with a Cause. In November of 1997, my AJ, a black Labrador Retriever came. She does many tasks (forty-three to be exact) for me. She opens doors, picks up dropped objects, brings me the phone, opens and closes the refrigerator. These are only a few tasks AJ can perform. But most of all she is great company for me. She helps me through daily tasks that before were out of reach. People still want to do for me, but I just remind them of my perfect AJ.[49]

Using Assistive Devices

Assistive devices, which are designed to help disabled people overcome their limitations, are another key to enhancing cerebral palsy patients' independence. Devices such as walkers and wheelchairs increase a person's mobility.

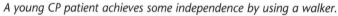

A young CP patient achieves some independence by using a walker.

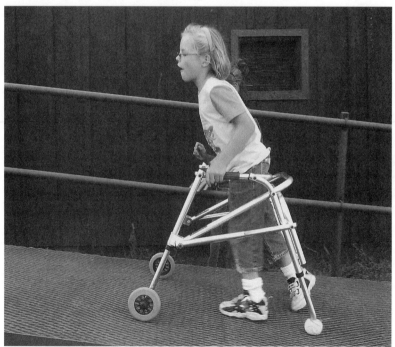

People who can walk but have poor balance often use a walker to help them to walk without falling. Walkers are made of light metal, such as aluminum, and have four legs and two handlebars. Unlike traditional walkers that surround a user's front and sides, these walkers surround a patient's back and sides, providing better balance. The user grasps the handlebars and takes a step, pulling the walker along. This helps patients get around more easily without depending on others to hold them up. A mother of a child with cerebral palsy says her son "could go almost anywhere with his walker. He loved the independence he had with it."[50]

Wheelchairs

For people with cerebral palsy who cannot walk, a wheelchair allows them to move from place to place independently. Special small wheelchairs are designed to accommodate children. Those individuals who have the use of their arms can propel themselves wherever the terrain is relatively flat and solid.

For people with limited use of their arms or hands, wheelchairs propelled by small electric motors are available. Motorized wheelchairs can be controlled by a handle or a joystick mounted on one armrest. This allows someone with minimal use of his or her hands to start, stop, steer, and turn the wheelchair easily. By helping them get around quickly and easily, motorized wheelchairs give people with even extreme levels of disability a sense of freedom, and this is the key to improving the quality of their lives. As one patient recalls, "I finally got my first electric [motorized] wheelchair in first grade. I was excited to have the freedom to roam around on my own. My dad remembers I took off immediately. I loved my newfound source of freedom."[51]

Although there is as yet no cure for cerebral palsy, with the help of assistive devices and supportive family, friends, and organizations, people with this disorder can overcome the challenges they face and lead happy, productive lives. Still, many look to the future, which they hope holds not just improved treatments for cerebral palsy symptoms but also a cure that will allow them to discard the assistive devices and fully partake of life as able-bodied persons.

Chapter 5

What the Future Holds

BECAUSE SCIENTISTS THINK that finding a cure for cerebral palsy will take many decades and, even when a cure is found, may be expensive and hard to administer, cerebral palsy research focuses on overcoming the disorder through prevention. Therefore, a number of studies are investigating ways to stop cerebral palsy from occurring. At the same time, in order to help people who have cerebral palsy now, scientists are developing new assistive devices to make living with the disorder easier.

Brain Development

Before they can determine how cellular development goes awry and causes cerebral palsy, scientists must first improve their understanding of normal brain cell development. By figuring out how brain cells form, how they specialize, and how they connect with each other and the rest of the body, scientists hope to gain insights into disruptions of this normal process. Researchers also hope to develop ways to prevent any disruption from occurring.

A number of studies now suggest that the abnormal brain cell development that can result in cerebral palsy is most likely to occur in the first few months of fetal growth. Since scientists know that brain cells develop during a certain period, they think monitoring brain cell development then will help prevent cerebral palsy.

The first three months of the fetus's life are crucial in the formation of the brain's motor centers. Thus, to prevent abnormal brain cell development, doctors monitor fetuses during this risky period for signs of stroke, oxygen deprivation, or exposure to

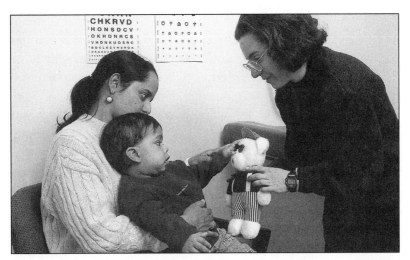

A mother holds her little boy, a CP patient, while they meet with a therapist who assesses his skills.

drugs and alcohol. In the past, such monitoring was difficult. To measure fetal brain activity, electrodes had to be inserted into the mother's scalp. However, scientists at the University of Arkansas are currently testing a less invasive monitoring device known as a fetal magnetoencephalograph (MEG). The fetal MEG makes monitoring easier because the pregnant woman needs only to lean against electronic sensors to pick up the fetus's brain activity. This allows doctors to detect abnormal brain activity and take steps to control the condition causing it before permanent damage occurs. According to a report from the Canadian Press, "The device could ultimately help doctors detect and treat conditions that might otherwise lead to mental retardation or other defects, such as cerebral palsy."[52]

Dangerous Events

At the same time, scientists are examining specific events, such as bleeding in the brain, that damage developing brain cells. Scientists hope that if they can learn exactly how such an event damages brain cells, they can develop ways to prevent the damage. For example, in one group of studies sponsored by the National Institute of Neurological Disorders and Stroke, scientists are investigating the relationship between bleeding in the brain and the release of a chemical known as glutamate. Research has shown that when bleeding in the brain occurs, abnormally large amounts of glutamate are produced. Scientists speculate that the high levels of glutamate can damage or destroy brain cells. Consequently, scientists are investigating how glutamate is released and what its effect on brain cells is. In the end, scientists hope to develop new drugs that can block the harmful effects, caused by the combination of bleeding in the brain and the release of glutamate.

Brain Mapping

While some scientists are studying early brain cell development, others are investigating fully developed brains in an effort to understand exactly how damaged cells produce the symptoms known as cerebral palsy. The first step in this line of inquiry is to devise a map of the brain that shows exactly which

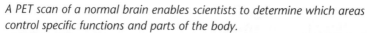

A PET scan of a normal brain enables scientists to determine which areas control specific functions and parts of the body.

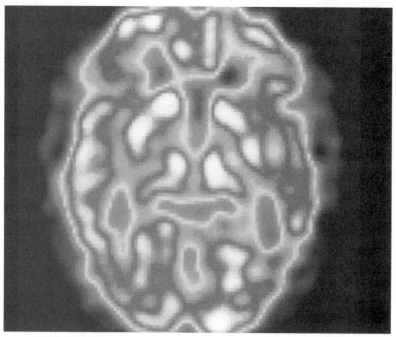

area is responsible for controlling specific actions and parts of the body. By doing this scientists hope to pinpoint brain areas that control specific movements, such as lifting an arm or leg, swallowing, or blinking an eye. Then they hope to compare brain activity in these areas between people with and without cerebral palsy to discover exactly what goes wrong in the brains of people with the disorder. If scientists can identify the differences in brain activity between healthy people and people with cerebral palsy and pinpoint specific areas of the brain that are responsible for particular actions, they may be able to develop effective methods to correct any abnormalities. This would prevent or even cure cerebral palsy.

Scientists have already been successful in using a positron-emission tomography (PET) scanner to make such a map. During a PET scan, subjects wear sensors on their heads; the sensors help scientists identify the parts of the brain that control certain movements. So far, scientists have been able to identify the sections of the brain that control balance, posture, and coordination. Scientists say that this knowledge will help them better understand and control ataxic cerebral palsy. Using PET scans, researchers have also identified the areas of the brain that control voluntary muscle movement and have located the exact spot where seizures begin. Scientists are now concentrating on modifying abnormalities in this spot in order to prevent seizures from occurring.

Scientists also hope to use PET scans and brain maps to track the effect of different treatments on the brains of people with cerebral palsy. Here, the goal is to understand why the treatments work and to evaluate their effectiveness. What researchers hope to gain is the ability to tailor treatment regimens to individual patient's needs. According to University of California, San Francisco, professor Nancy Bly, "You can treat the muscular imbalance, alignment problems and all the mechanical events, but you've got to consider the whole person and how the problem is stored in the nervous system. We have such an incredible opportunity to take what we learn in neuroscience [brain mapping] and apply it to physical therapy."[53]

Investigating Low Birth Weight

Not all cerebral palsy research is focused on the brain. Since many premature and low-birth-weight babies develop cerebral palsy, researchers are also examining what factors encourage premature births and low birth weight and how to prevent these factors from occurring.

Scientists know that infection with toxoplasmosis bacteria, rubella, and cytomegalovirus can affect brain cell development and encourage premature birth. Accordingly, scientists are examining whether there are other bacteria and viruses that cause the same response. They are particularly interested in the bacteria that cause periodontal or gum infections. In 2001 research conducted jointly at the University of North Carolina, Chapel Hill, and at Duke University in Durham, North Carolina, found that one in five premature babies is born to a mother with a periodontal infection. And the worse the infection is, the more likely the mother is to give birth to a premature baby. Since practicing good dental hygiene can prevent gum infections, this is a risk factor that scientists say can easily be eliminated. According to Duke University researcher Steven Offenbacher,

> One of the major problems in preventing premature births is the causes and complications of pregnancy and neonatal illness are not fully understood. The significance of this work is that these findings may eventually have a dramatic impact on health care, because unlike many risk factors, periodontal disease is both preventable and treatable.[54]

Similarly, scientists are also using what they know about the connection between smoking and cerebral palsy to examine whether exposure to environmental or secondhand smoke, can lead to premature births. In a study at Ulleval University Hospital in Oslo, Norway, scientists investigated whether secondhand smoke effects premature births. To do this, researchers tested the hair follicles of nonsmoking pregnant women for nicotine, a chemical found in tobacco smoke. Those women who were exposed to the most secondhand tobacco smoke had the largest concentration of nicotine in their hair. Correspondingly, they

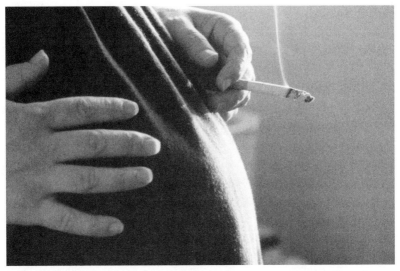

A pregnant smoker may be responsible for giving birth prematurely and putting her baby at risk for CP.

were three times more likely to give birth to premature infants than the subjects who were not exposed to smoke. Based on the results of this study, scientists believe that exposure to second-hand smoke can cause premature births. To prevent cerebral palsy and other problems caused by premature births, groups such as the National Institute of Environmental Health Science are lobbying state and local governments to pass laws that will prohibit cigarette smoking in public areas.

Magnesium and Birth Weight

In addition to the effects of secondhand smoke, scientists are ex-amining specific dietary factors in an effort to reduce the number of premature births. One of the most promising areas of research centers around magnesium, a mineral found in many foods, in-cluding beans, whole grain cereals, and green vegetables. Doctors have observed that treatment with magnesium ends premature labor and delays premature births. Therefore, experts have con-cluded that expectant mothers who are deficient in magnesium are more likely to experience premature labor. Moreover, even when treatment with magnesium does not prevent premature births, low-birth-weight infants are less likely to develop cerebral palsy if their mothers are treated with magnesium shortly before giving birth. Consequently, scientists theorize that a lack of magnesium may negatively affect brain cell development in infants and lead to the development of cerebral palsy.

In 1995, in an effort to test this theory, scientists in California compared the incidence of cerebral palsy in premature infants whose mothers received treatment with magnesium to those who did not. The study found that the infants whose mothers were treated with magnesium were 25 percent less likely to develop cerebral palsy than the infants whose mothers were not treated with magnesium. According to a report by the National Institute of Neurological Disorders and Stroke, "Low birth weight babies are 100 times more likely to develop CP than normal birth weight infants. Use of magnesium sulfate may prevent 25 percent of the cases of CP in the approximately 52,000 low birth weight babies born each year in the United States."[55]

Although scientists are unsure why magnesium helps prevent cerebral palsy, they do know that chemicals in the brain known

Magnesium, a mineral found in foods such as green vegetables, shows promise in reducing the number of premature births.

as neurotransmitters need magnesium to function properly. Therefore, they theorize that a lack of magnesium may cause abnormalities in the development of neurotransmitters, as well as in brain cells, causing cerebral palsy.

Life-Enhancing Technology

Scientists hope that greater understanding of the causes of cerebral palsy will help prevent the disorder, but they are also working on developing new and more effective assistive devices to help cerebral palsy patients now. Much of this research involves the use of technology and includes state-of-the-art wheelchairs. One such wheelchair, under development, allows its user to stand upright. Known as an upright mobility scooter, this wheelchair is narrower than a traditional wheelchair. It can rise up, stand on two wheels, and lift its occupant into a standing position. Research has found that standing upright is good for the circulatory system, improves digestion, and strengthens bones and muscles. In addition, being able to stand has psychological benefits. It permits wheelchair users to meet with and talk to nondisabled people face to face. As one cerebral palsy patient says,

> It would be awesome to be able to look people straight in the eye when I talk to them. Because I'm in a wheelchair, it makes me seem small. People talk to me as if I'm a child instead of a woman. I'd sure like to be able to look right at people when I talk to them instead of me being down here and them being way up there. I think the difference makes some people feel superior.[56]

Other scientists are working on even more versatile wheelchairs. One, which is similar in design to the standing wheelchair, will be able to climb up and down stairs easily. It uses a stabilizing device, called a gyrostabilizer to keep the wheelchair from tipping over. Such a wheelchair would make daily living for people with cerebral palsy easier and more like the lives of able-bodied people because it would provide the same type of access to multistoried buildings. According to experts at Infinitec, Inc., a nonprofit corporation formed to help people with disabilities access new assistive devices, "All through time, beginning with the invention of the wheel, the disability community has merged with the mainstream to live the best life possible. Twenty-first century scientists mean to blur the disability distinction altogether with wheelchairs that climb stairs."[57]

Sports Wheelchairs

Other new wheelchairs are designed to help people with cerebral palsy who want to participate in indoor and outdoor sports. A number of specialized sports wheelchairs are already on the market, with others in development. Two wheelchairs already on the market include racing wheelchairs and all-terrain wheelchairs. Racing wheelchairs, also called high-performance wheelchairs, are like ten-speed bicycles; they have gears that allow the user to increase the chair's speed. These manual wheelchairs are ultralight, fast, and extremely maneuverable. These wheelchairs include features such as swing-away arms, rear anti-tippers, and a basketball holder. They can also be customized and modified to suit the individual user and the sport in which he or she is participating.

All-terrain wheelchairs are similar to mountain bikes. More rugged than traditional wheelchairs, these wheelchairs have special large tires that allow them to move easily over sand, mud, gravel, and snow. All-terrain wheelchairs give users easy access to places that are difficult to visit in a traditional wheelchair, such as beaches, forests, and snowy areas. Such wheelchairs also allow people, who could otherwise not do so, to participate in more varied outdoor activities and enjoy more active lives. A patient who uses an all-terrain wheelchair explains, "It goes over unpaved surfaces well, and is great for outdoor activities where a power chair cannot go."[58]

New Computers

Other technology uses computers to make living with cerebral palsy easier. A head-tracking mouse, for example, is an alternative to a head pointer because it permits people who have limited use of their hands to control a computer without wearing a bulky head pointer. A head-tracking mouse consists of two wireless optical sensors. One, which resembles a small eye, is perched on the

A mother and her two children, one afflicted with CP, spend an idyllic afternoon at the beach. Her older son uses an all-terrain wheelchair.

top of a computer monitor. The other, which is no bigger than a dot, is attached to the wearer's forehead or eyeglasses and acts like a reflector. The sensor on the monitor transmits a signal to the sensor that the user wears. When users move their heads, that movement is tracked by the sensors and converted into direct movements of the cursor on the screen. Thus, turning one's head to the right directs the cursor to move right. By combining the head-tracking mouse with newly developed on-screen keyboards, people with limited mobility can use personal computers to communicate. In particular they can send and receive email more easily. Such computers are already on the market.

Robotics

Research into even greater application of computer technology continues. Among the most interesting projects scientists are working on to assist people with cerebral palsy are robots programmed to perform tasks that might otherwise be difficult for persons with disabilities. One robot in development, a robotic dog, is mounted on wheels and has a video camera for eyes. The video camera is connected to a voice synthesizer. Programmed with the ability to read and speak, the robotic dog uses its video camera to read messages its owner writes and then, via the synthesizer, speaks the messages aloud. This provides a voice for patients with speech impairments. In addition, the dog can be outfitted with a global positioning system and a mapping program that enables it to guide its user to unfamiliar places. For people who cannot have a live service dog, whether due to allergies, living arrangements that do not allow animals, or an inability to care for an animal, a robotic dog has many advantages.

Other robots under development are being programmed to do a number of everyday tasks, including cleaning house, washing dishes, fetching useful items, taking memos, and word processing,

Robotic devices such as this vacuum cleaner assist CP patients with daily tasks, substantially decreasing their reliance on other people.

in an effort to make life easier for people with cerebral palsy. According to experts at Infinitec, "Research at many universities will soon lead to the development of assistive robots for performing everyday tasks. One of the most important future applications of intelligent physical robots is to assist people in their physical manipulation of the world."[59]

Cybernetics

For some of the researchers who design assistive devices, the ultimate goal is to create devices that require no direct manipulation of controls by the user but are instead controlled by a computer and by the user's mind. Such science is called cybernetics. Currently, scientists are developing cybernetic assistive devices that are controlled by microchips implanted directly into the brains of people with neurological disabilities, including cerebral palsy. The job of these microchips is to correct distorted signals produced by damaged parts of the brain. Scientists theorize that by programming a computer to send and receive messages to and from the microchips, they can use electrical activity in the brain to control a robotic limb that would take the place of a disabled limb. In this way, scientists predict, people with neurological disabilities will someday be able to think of a body movement and move a robotic arm or leg accordingly.

Some recent experiments suggest that this goal is within reach. In 2000, at Duke University in North Carolina, scientists implanted tiny wires into the brain of a monkey. The wires were also connected to a computer, which converted the electrical activity coming from the monkey's brain to a mechanical arm in another room and, via the Internet, to a second mechanical arm six hundred miles away at the Massachusetts Institute of Technology. The scientists hypothesized that when the monkey moved its arm, the electrical activity in the monkey's brain that caused his arm to move would also move the two mechanical arms.

To test this theory, the monkey was taught to use its right arm to move a joystick as it watched a group of lights on a monitor. If the monkey moved the joystick the way the scientists wanted it to, lights appeared on the monitor and a dispenser sent a drop of juice into the animal's mouth. As the monkey moved its arm, the computer transmitted the electrical impulses generated in the monkey's brain to the two mechanical arms. As the scientists had expected, when the monkey moved its arm to the right, the mechanical arms also moved to the right.

Next, the scientists disabled the connection between the joystick and the lights on the computer monitor. Now, the monkey had to rely solely on its brain activity to move the lights. Although the monkey continued to move its arm at first, after a while it was able to control the lights by brain activity alone. Scientists hope to add the mechanical arms to this study in the future, and they predict that the monkey will be able to move the mechanical arms with its mind in the same manner.

Scientists want to use what they learn from this study to do two things. First, they hope to create robotic limbs that people with neurological disorders can control with their brains. They also think that, eventually, they will be able to connect the microchips in patients' brains to the muscles in their disabled limbs, essentially replacing the damaged motor centers of the brain. According to Duke University scientists, "Our immediate goal is to help a person who has been paralyzed by a neurological disorder [such as cerebral palsy] to operate a robotic limb. Someday the research could also help such a patient regain control over a natural arm or leg with the aid of wireless communication between the brain and the limb."[60]

Until that time comes, people with cerebral palsy are taking advantage of new assistive devices as they look hopefully to the future. Their overall hope is for this disabling condition to be a distant memory, for people to live full and independent lives unimpeded by clumsy equipment. As one young woman with cerebral palsy explains, "My life isn't perfect. But whose life is? But despite my problems, I'm enjoying my life. Of course, I wish I could walk, and I pray that they will come up with a cure for CP someday. Scientists are doing some incredible work. Anything can happen."[61]

Notes

Introduction: A Misunderstood Disorder
1. Amanda, interview by author, Dallas, Texas, October 1, 2002.
2. Amanda, interview.
3. Amanda, interview.

Chapter 1: What Is Cerebral Palsy?
4. Danny, interview by author, Fort Worth, Texas, September 20, 2002.
5. Kathy Stone-Kojis, "Do Something, Something's Wrong with My Baby!" www.Cpconnection.com.
6. Marie A. Kennedy, *My Perfect Son Has Cerebral Palsy*. Bloomington, IN: First Books Library, 2001, p. 33.
7. Shelley Nixon, *From Where I Sit*. New York: Scholastic, 1999, p. 29.
8. Danny, interview.
9. Monica Videnieks, "Communication Not Lacking in This Relationship," *Accent on Living*, Summer 2001, p. 66.
10. Freeman Miller and Steven Bachrach, *Cerebral Palsy: A Complete Guide for Caregiving*. Baltimore. Johns Hopkins University Press, 1995, p. 9.
11. Nixon, *From Where I Sit*, p. 6.
12. Danny, interview.
13. Neurology Channel, "Cerebral Palsy," www.neurology channel.com.

Chapter 2: Diagnosis and Treatment
14. Yvette, interview by author, Dallas,Texas, September 28, 2002.
15. Yvette, interview.
16. Ozana Pope-Gajic, "Children and Physical Therapy I." www. suite 101.com.

17. Kennedy, *My Perfect Son Has Cerebral Palsy*, p. 24.
18. Wai Kin Chiu, "My Left Knee." www.tell-us-your-story.com.
19. Danny, interview.
20. Rhonda, interview by author, Dallas, Texas, October 2, 2002.
21. Chiu, "My Left Knee."
22. Yvette, interview.
23. Kennedy, *My Perfect Son Has Cerebral Palsy*, p. 26.
24. Quoted in Children's Hemiplegia and Stroke Association, "Orthotics." www.chasa.org.

Chapter 3: Alternative Treatments

25. Quoted in Laura Shapiro Kramer, *Uncommon Voyage*. Boston: Faber & Faber, 1996, p. xi.
26. Andrew Vickers, *Health Options: Complementary Therapies for Cerebral Palsy and Related Conditions*. Rockport, ME: Element, 1994, p. 16.
27. Quoted in The Healing Center Online, "Chiropractic Care and CP Management." www.healing-arts.org.
28. Kramer, *Uncommon Voyage*, p. 115.
29. Wei Wen, "Ancient Paralysing Art Modified to Cure Paralysis." www.users.bigpond.net.au.
30. Quoted in Bioneurofeedback, "Biofeedback/Neurofeedback Therapy." www.bioneurofeedback.com.
31. Association for Applied Psychophysiology and Biofeedback, "What Is Biofeedback?" www.aapb.org.
32. Yoga and the Special Child, "Cerebral Palsy and Yoga." www.specialyoga.com.
33. Danny, interview.
34. Kramer, *Uncommon Voyage*, p. 99.
35. Quoted in Jean Paul Collett et al., "Hyperbaric Oxygen for Children with Cerebral Palsy: A Randomised Multicentre Trial," *The Lancet*, vol. 357, no. 9256, February 24, 2001, p. 582.
36. Danny, interview.

Chapter 4: Living with Cerebral Palsy

37. Amanda, interview.
38. Quoted in Kristi Arellano, "Denver Architects, Builders Open Doors for Disabled," *Denver Post*, May 13, 2001, p. K1.

39. Quoted in Arellano, "Denver Architects, Builders Open Doors for Disabled."

40. Amanda, interview.

41. Amanda, interview.

42. Quoted in Monica Videnieks, "Palsy Victim Enthralls Court," *Australian*, March 15, 2001, p. 3.

43. Quoted in Rosemarie Blitchington, "King of the Canvas," *We-Media*, September/October 2000, p. 34.

44. Danny, interview.

45. Amanda, interview.

46. UCP Houston, "Summer Camps." www.ucphouston.org.

47. Amanda, interview.

48. Nixon, *From Where I Sit*, p. 4.

49. Quoted in Angelfire.com, "AJ: The Perfect Dog." www.angelfire.com.

50. Kennedy, *My Perfect Son Has Cerebral Palsy*, p. 38.

51. Nixon, *From Where I Sit*, p. 38.

Chapter 5: What the Future Holds

52. Monica Videnieks, Canadian Press, "Vancouver-Area Firm Builds a Device to Measure Fetal Brain Signals," June 27, 2000.

53. Quoted in Sue Goetinck Ambrose, "Blueprint for the Brain," *Dallas Morning News*, December 24, 2000, p. 7D.

54. Quoted in University of North Carolina, "News." www.unc.edu

55. National Institute of Neurological Disorders and Stroke, "Magnesium Sulfate and Decreased Risk of Cerebral Palsy." www.ninds.nih.gov.

56. Amanda, interview.

57. Infinitec, "Salute to Technology." www.infinitec.org.

58. Quoted in Jason Marine Enterprises, Inc., "Go and Explore Your World." www.jmseeker.com.

59. Infinitec, "Robotics and Cybernetics." www.infinitec.org.

60. Miguel Nicolelis and John Chapin, "Controlling Robots with the Mind," *Scientific American*, October 2002, p. 46.

61. Amanda, interview.

Glossary

antibodies: Infection-fighting substances produced by the body's immune system.

anticholinergic drugs: Drugs that control involuntary muscle movement.

assistive device: A tool, such as a wheelchair, that helps make life easier for a disabled person.

ataxic cerebral palsy: A type of cerebral palsy causing problems with balance and coordination.

athetoid cerebral palsy: A type of cerebral palsy in which affected muscles move involuntarily.

bilirubin: A toxic chemical produced when blood cells break down.

CAT scan: A computerized, 3-D X ray.

chiropractic treatment: An alternative treatment that involves the applying of mild force to the spine in order to relieve pressure on nearby nerves.

cybernetics: The science of automatic control systems.

diazepam: A drug used to relax tight muscles.

diplegia: The inability to move either both arms or both legs.

fetus: An unborn baby.

glutamate: A chemical produced by the brain in large amounts when bleeding occurs and that may damage developing brain cells.

hemiplegia: The inability to move the arm and leg on one side of the body.

jaundice: A condition in which components of bile build up in the bloodstream.

motor skills: The ability to move the body.

neurotransmitters: Chemicals in the brain that permit messages to travel from brain cell to brain cell.

occupational therapist: A trained professional who helps people with cerebral palsy develop control of their small muscles.

occupational therapy: A treatment for cerebral palsy that is designed to help patients improve control of their small muscles.

orthotist: A professional who makes braces and casts.

PET scan: Also known as a positron-emission tomography scan; a specialized computer picture of an internal organ like the brain.

physical therapist: A trained professional who helps people with cerebral palsy develop control of their large muscles.

physical therapy: A treatment for cerebral palsy that is designed to help patients improve control of their large muscles.

premature birth: Birth that occurs before the end of the normal forty-week-long pregnancy.

quadriplegia: The inability to move all four limbs.

Rh factor: A chemical found in the blood of people with type 0+, A+, B+, and AB+ blood.

spastic cerebral palsy: A type of cerebral palsy causing stiff and severely cramped muscles.

speech pathologist: A trained professional who diagnoses and helps correct speech impairments.

speech therapy: A form of treatment that helps people to speak more clearly and easily.

static disorder: A disorder that neither worsens nor improves.

Organizations to Contact

Canine Companions for Independence
PO Box 446
2965 Dutton Ave.
Santa Rosa, CA 95402-0446
(707) 577-1700
email: info@caninecompanions.org
This organization trains dogs to assist handicapped people and pairs up people with the dogs.

Children's Hemiplegia and Stroke Association
4101 W. Green Oaks Blvd., PMB #149
Arlington, TX 76016
(817) 492-4325
website: www.hemikids.org
The association offers information and support about hemiplegia and sponsors research into the disorder.

National Easter Seals Society
230 W. Monroe St.
Chicago, IL 60606-4802
(800) 221-6827
website: www.easter-seals.org
This society provides rehabilitation and support services throughout the United States, offers information about cerebral palsy, and helps in obtaining assistive devices. It sponsors research, camps, social clubs, and helps people gain access to special transportation.

National Sports Center for the Disabled
PO Box 1290
Winter Park, CO 80482
(970) 726-1540
email: info@nscd.org

This group sponsors sports competitions for physically challenged people. It provides information on parks and campgrounds that are accessible to the handicapped.

North American Riding for the Handicapped Association
PO Box 33150
Denver, CO 80233
(800) 369-7433
website: www.narha.org

The association provides information on therapeutic horseback riding, including lists of centers throughout the United States.

Therapeutic Golf Foundation
(205) 980-1911

This organization helps connect disabled people with special golf programs throughout the United States.

United Cerebral Palsy Association
1660 L St. NW, Suite 700
Washington, DC 20036
(800) 872-5827
website: www.ucpa.org

This association provides information and support for people with cerebral palsy and their families. It sponsors research and camps and publishes informational pamphlets. There are many local chapters of the association throughout the United States.

For Further Reading

Books

Nathan Aaseng, *Cerebral Palsy*. New York: Franklin Watts, 1991. A comprehensive but easy-to-read book that discusses the causes and treatment of cerebral palsy and examines what it is like to grow up with the disorder.

Laura Anne Gilman, *Coping with Cerebral Palsy*. New York: Rosen, 2001. A young adult talks about ways teenagers can cope with cerebral palsy. The book discusses social, workplace, legal, and educational issues.

Elizabeth Helfman, *On Being Sarah*. Morton Grove, IL: Albert Whitman, 1992. A novel about a young woman with cerebral palsy who cannot walk or speak.

Don Pincus, *Everything You Need to Know About Cerebral Palsy*. New York: Rosen, 2000. An easy-to-read book that looks at the causes, diagnosis, treatment of, and problems of living with cerebral palsy.

Websites

Association for Applied Psychophysiology and Biofeedback (www.aapb.org). The association provides information on biofeedback.

CP Connection (www.cpconnection.com). This site gives information and support to people with cerebral palsy. It provides chat rooms and message boards and helps people with cerebral palsy connect with each other.

Infinitec (www.infinitec.org). Infinitec gives information on high-tech assistive devices.

Jason Marine Enterprises, Inc. (www.jmseeker.com). This company manufactures and sells a number of specially designed wheelchairs for athletes with cerebral palsy.

National Institute of Neurological Disorders and Stroke (www.ninds.nih.gov). The institute provides information on disorders caused by brain cell damage and stroke.

Tell Us Your Story (www.tell-us-your-story.com). This website features true stories by people with cerebral palsy about how they have overcome the challenges they face.

Works Consulted

Books

Marie A. Kennedy, *My Perfect Son Has Cerebral Palsy*. Bloomington, IN: First Books Library, 2001. The mother of a cerebral palsy patient talks about the challenges her son faces and how the family is coping.

Laura Shapiro Kramer, *Uncommon Voyage*. Boston: Faber & Faber, 1996. This book focuses on different alternative treatments for cerebral palsy and the effects the treatments had on the author's son.

Freeman Miller and Steven Bachrach, *Cerebral Palsy: A Complete Guide for Caregiving*. Baltimore: Johns Hopkins University Press, 1995. The authors present a wealth of information on the types of cerebral palsy and the different treatments and assistive devices available.

Shelley Nixon, *From Where I Sit*. New York: Scholastic, 1999. A young woman with cerebral palsy talks about her life.

Andrew Vickers, *Health Options: Complementary Therapies for Cerebral Palsy and Related Conditions*. Rockport, ME: Element, 1994. This book discusses a wide range of alternative treatments for cerebral palsy.

Periodicals

Sue Goetinck Ambrose, "Blueprint for the Brain," *Dallas Morning News*, December 24, 2000.

Kristi Arellano, "Denver Architects, Builders Open Doors for Disabled," *Denver Post*, May 13, 2001.

Rosemarie Blitchington, "King of the Canvas," *WeMedia*, September/October 2000.

Jean Paul Collett, "Hyperbaric Oxygen for Children with Cerebral Palsy: A Randomised Multicentre Trial," *The Lancet,* vol. 357, no. 9256, February 24, 2001.

Miguel Nicolelis and John Chapin, "Controlling Robots with the Mind," *Scientific American,* October 2002.

Monica Videnieks, "Communication Not Lacking in This Relationship," *Accent on Living,* Summer 2001.

———, "Palsy Victim Enthralls Court," *Australian,* March 15, 2001.

———, "Vancouver-Area Firm Builds a Device to Measure Fetal Brain Signals," *Canadian Press,* June 27, 2000.

Internet Sources

Angelfire, "AJ: The Perfect Dog," www.angelfire.com.

Association for Applied Psychophysiology and Biofeedback, "What Is Biofeedback?" www.aapb.org.

Bioneurofeedback, "Biofeedback/Neurofeedback Therapy." www.bioneurofeedback.com.

Children's Hemiplegia and Stroke Association, "Orthotics." www.chasa.org.

Wai Kin Chiu, "My Left Knee." www.tell-us-your-story.com.

Sanjay Gupta, "On Their Own Two Feet." www.time.com.

Healing Center Online, "Chiropractic Care and CP Management." www.healing-arts.org.

Infinitec, "Robotics and Cybernetics." www.infinitec.org.

———, "Salute to Technology." www.infinitec.org.

Jason Marine Enterprises, Inc., "Go and Explore Your World." www.jmseeker.com.

National Institute of Neurological Disorders and Stroke, "Magnesium Sulfate and Decreased Risk of Cerebral Palsy." www.ninds.nih.gov.

Neurology Channel, "Cerebral Palsy." www.neurology-channel.com.

Ozana Pope-Gajic, "Children and Physical Therapy I." www.suite101.com.

Kathy Stone-Kojis, "Do Something, Something's Wrong with My Baby!" www.Cpconnection.com.

UCP Houston, "Summer Camps." www.ucphouston.org.

University of North Carolina, "News." www.unc.edu.

Wei Wen, "Ancient Paralysing Art Modified to Cure Paralysis." www.users.bigpond.net.au.

Yoga and the Special Child, "Cerebral Palsy and Yoga." www.specialyoga.com.

Index

Picture Credits

About the Author

Barbara Sheen has been a writer and educator for more than thirty years. She writes in both English and Spanish. Her fiction and nonfiction books have been published in the United States and Europe. She currently lives in Texas with her family, where she enjoys swimming, weight training, reading, and cooking. This is her sixth book in Lucent's Diseases and Disorders series.